DATE DUE

and
one
more
thing...

joan caraganis jakobson

and

one

more

thing...

a mother's
advice
on life,
love, and
lipstick

WARNER BOOKS

NEW YORK   BOSTON

WARNER BOOKS

Time Warner Book Group
1271 Avenue of the Americas, New York, NY 10020
Visit our Web site at www.twbookmark.com.

Printed in the United States of America

First Printing: April 2005
10 9 8 7 6 5 4 3 2 1

Library of Congress Cataloging-in-Publication Data
Jakobson, Joan Caraganis.
    And one more thing— : a mother's advice on life, love and lipstick /
Joan Caraganis Jakobson. — 1st ed.
        p. cm.
     ISBN 0-446-57669-7
   1. Mothers and daughters. 2. Conduct of life. I. Title.
    HQ755.85.J333 2005
    306.874'3—dc22   2004019570

Book design by rlf design
Illustrations by Chesley McLaren

to my mother, jane welt,

who informed me when I was seventeen that
if I insisted on staying out past my curfew,
I would be considered a Glad Girl. Years later, when
I asked her exactly what a "Glad Girl" was, she said
she had no idea and had made it up on the spot. She
taught me that when you are the mother of a
daughter, you use whatever works.

and to all the future
glad girls

acknowledgments

Even know-it-all mothers need occasional guidance, and I was splendidly attended to by many friends. Suzanne Jones Maas, Kevin Abernathy, Didi Fenton Schafer, Maggie McLean, Suzanne O'Malley, Jurate Kazickas, Deborah Krulewitch, Anna Quindlen, Joanie McDonell, Louise Mirrer, Barbara Lazear Ascher, Jennifer Vaughan Maanavi, Anne Greene, Marianne Diorio, Michael LaRocca, Scott Briggs, David Patrick Columbia, Betty Prashker, Samantha Topping, and Lily Shapovalov very kindly shared their insights and wisdom with me.

My friend and agent, Robin Straus, was not only unfailingly supportive on this project but was also the best lunch companion. Amy Einhorn, my editor at Warner Books, who seems much too young to be so smart and understanding, was joy to work with, as was Todd Doughty, my wonderfully bright and charming publicist.

To my sweet and fearless Nicholas, who has turned out remarkably well in spite of, or perhaps because of the fact that I have very little advice for grown sons. To my husband, John, for his unending patience and

acknowledgments

assistance on this book (particularly in the finance and sports sections) and with whom I finally got it right. And to my Caitlin, who in spite of it all, is still speaking to me.

foreword

by Wendy Wasserstein

When a young woman graduates from college today, chances are she has dissected a frog, she has perfected one foreign language, mastered basic calculus, and is familiar with the first twelve lines of the *Canterbury Tales*. These are all important accomplishments, but not necessarily helpful when it's time to buy your first sofa. This simple aqua book answers all the questions young women really want the answers to but are afraid to ask.

From dating to dinner parties, Joan Jakobson offers twenty-first-century homespun wisdom. She is sophisticated, but warm. She is knowing, yet ironic. There are no recipes here for Ritz cracker pies and Swedish meatballs. The days of waiting to be pinned and then engaged are, thank god, over. No one is going to go to Sunday brunch in white gloves unless it's for the Halloween parade in Greenwich Village. Now, in the aftermath of a happy destruction of all these formal rules, the question of what to do and when still emerges.

Shows about single women, like *Sex in the City*, have guided new generations of single women with depictions of friendship, social mores, and fashion. But when you get right down to it, knowing that five-inch Manolo Blahnik heels are in isn't going to help you set the table for a dinner party, or advise you what the hell to do when the person sitting next to you is a complete bore. Joan Jakobson offers keen advice for the new basics. She is not only post-feminist, she is post-chic.

This book is gloriously reasonable and honest. Joan's answers to questions like what to do when a friend borrows money or what is the difference between dating a W.A.S.P. and a Jewish man are refreshingly frank. It's as if one is talking to a mother, older sister, and best friend who is nonjudgmental and consistently offers do-able solutions. It's impossible to read any of Joan's life answers and not think, "This is wise, *and* I won't have to overhaul my life to execute it."

So much of a young woman's life has been turned over to media images of six-foot, 110lb girls who are Harvard Law graduates and celebrity models, who just moved into their *InStyle* magazine three-bedroom house in Laurel Canyon, where they exercise three hours a day, make over a million dollars a year, and look forward to getting their figure back within a week if they ever have a baby. These images can only make real women feel diminished about themselves and their accomplishments. They have nothing to do with the real-life difficulties of getting the first apartment, decorating it, or even cooking in it. Joan Jakobson addresses these issues with dignity. Her advice is not for a fantasy life but is clearly the result of her own experiences as a mother and a working writer.

The questions and answers in this book are not the final word on romance, dieting, or decorating. The best possible outcome to a daughter or a mother reading this practical handbook is to open up an intergenerational dialogue. At a time in which social mores, especially for women, are in a state of flux, guidebooks like this one offer an intelligent way to navigate everything from day-to-day events to important life choices. So much of the literature written for women is about "should"s. Formerly, the validity of a woman's life hinged on domesticity. Since then, we've come a long way, baby, and we've been told we should have it all. Most recently, the message has been added to, so that young women should have a perfect domestic life, a perfect work life, plus perfect bodies and perfect sex lives. All of these "should"s cloud our ability to deal with the basic challenges that life presents to us. Whether you agree with Joan Jakobson's solutions or not, one must respect her attempts to address the realities of a young woman's life.

I remember leafing through books like *Tiffany's*

Table Manners for Teenagers or *Amy Vanderbilt's Etiquette Book* when I was in high school and thinking, "These are intriguing anthropological studies into a foreign species." Frankly, finger bowls weren't very common in my high school. I secretly wanted to know which fork to use for fish and what to do with a used napkin. But I never dared to mention it out loud. And yet, when I came of age and began going to dinner with a man who offered to pay for the meal, I wished those etiquette books had offered some guidance about when it was appropriate to accept and when I should offer to go Dutch.

Joan Jakobson does not shy away from these or any other delicate subjects. She candidly discusses her own marriages and romances. She is not a goody-goody, and she doesn't fall for easy self-help answers either. Unlike the current trend of narcissistic self-revelation, her advice is often pro-active. Her advice on life, love, and lipstick is often to figure out a way to get on with it as gracefully and pragmatically as possible.

introduction for mothers . . . and daughters

I realize that from the sixth grade until college graduation (and yes, sometimes even beyond) most daughters are in profound denial that any maternal advice
can be even remotely valuable or worth listening to. It
wasn't until I was nearly out of college when I realized
that much of my mother's advice actually made remarkably good sense. With each turning point in my
adult life—marriages, babies, divorces, boring men at
dinner parties—it was, ultimately, her rules and advice about manners and behavior that saw me through.
I didn't agree on every single issue that she feels
strongly about, but she provided a sturdy, reliable
framework for me and I would like to do the same for
my daughter.

I began writing this book several years ago when
my daughter, Caitlin, and some of her college friends
were visiting and we chatted away on a drizzly gray
summer weekend. I was amazed that they wanted to
talk with me for more than five minutes. (Of course, if
the sun had been shining and they could have gone to

the beach, I would have been alone in the kitchen, talking to myself as I emptied the dishwasher.) But as we began discussions on the usual topics, I found myself beginning sentences with, "Now when you girls get married . . ." and "Of course, when you have children of your own, I hope you'll never . . ." And I was pleasantly astonished when the girls actually seemed interested in what I was telling them. (Caitlin hadn't asked me for advice since she was in the second grade and wanted to know how to get rid of a cowlick in her eyebrow, a little-known affliction, then and now.) The heartening memory of that day was the fact that they not only welcomed some direction, but also the knowledge that rules, though ever changing, still exist.

Since the starting point of this book was a series of questions and answers among my child, her friends, and me, I have stuck to that arrangement. Caitlin, who represents our universal daughter, poses the questions and I, the collective mother, attempt to answer them. When Caitlin recently announced her engagement, I realized that I had plenty to tell her before she left home for good, and there wasn't much time left before the rehearsal dinner.

Even though I wrote this for daughters, my friends who have read it found it useful. Of course, they didn't agree with me on every topic (not many do), but reading it helped them figure out just what it was they wanted to tell their daughters. For those mothers who want to modify or adapt this book for their own girls, there are several blank pages at the end where they can add their own recommendations and tell their family stories. These pages will also provide mothers with the opportunity to offer some maternal advice that can be read and absorbed by their daughters in private. These same mothers will be spared a face-to-face discussion and the subsequent rolling of eyes, accompanied by a chorus of "Oh, please!" and cell phones conveniently ringing the minute a new subject is launched.

For the girls, the good news is I'm not their mother. The bad news is I have even more to say than she does. But maybe because they'll never have to face me at the dinner table, they'll listen.

Despite the fact that, according to some, I look like a middle-aged woman from the suburbs who drives a minivan, my life did not always proceed on a proper course. After Caitlin's father and I divorced when she was five years old, I fell in love with a married man and had a baby boy with him before his divorce was final. During this time, I had the deeply dubious distinction of being the first unwed, pregnant class mother in the history of my daughter's very traditional school. However, because I wrote my thank-you notes promptly and never wore a T-shirt that said "Beer Is Food" to the Middle School Parents' Night Dinner, everyone survived. (Except my father.)

The impression I hope that you ultimately take away from this book is that the social graces, our codes of behavior, have endured because they work. Over the years, although we've tweaked the rules, we've kept them close by our side because by following them, we gain the freedom to deal with unforeseen issues. Events occur that are part of the human condition, but for which no one can plan. But etiquette codes can ease the journey. Master the minor issues and you can deal with the important subjects on your own terms.

Of course, I will tell daughters what to do about a host of other things that may occur as they get older, such as living on their own for the first time, financial concerns, dating, parties and men, careers, future husband, and future children.

And I will also give advice on how to respond if you see your best friend's husband with another woman, how to tip hotel concierges, and the importance of using a lash primer before applying mascara. These subjects may seem rather trivial now but learning more about them can help you keep your friends happy, avoid the loser rooms in hotels, and make your eyelashes look improbably thick and wavy without having to resort to a scary eyelash curler.

Our girls are leaving home to begin their new adventures, so we'd better make sure they're prepared for life without us—whether it's marriage or graduate school, a career in bartending or weaving classes in Guatemala. Even if they don't follow our advice immediately—with this book, it will be available for them to act upon at some later date, especially if they hope to inherit any jewelry.

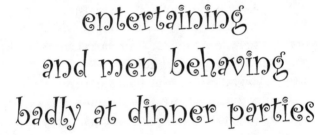

1

entertaining
and men behaving
badly at dinner parties

and one more thing . . .

Mommy, shouldn't you begin this book by discussing how to live on your own for the first time? But then, why would I expect the conventional response from you? Okay, why do you always say, "Never pass up a party"?

Because you never know who you might meet. If you do go to a party and find that it's a bust, you can always leave, but if you don't go at all, you will spend the next week listening to friends describe the best night they ever had and maybe the next year wondering what or who might have been if you had fixed your hair and gone.

I think that the more often I go out in the evening, the thinner I become. When I stay in at night, I have dinner and then sit in front of the television with a book or magazine. I find myself going into the kitchen every ten or fifteen minutes for something to eat. When I'm out, I have dinner and don't snack away during the hours between dinner and bed. I don't share this discovery with many people because I sound like an airhead, but I think it's the truth.

Whatever. Move on.

Okay, party specifics. Let's start with the invitations. A majority of birthday party invitations I now receive include the words "No Presents

2

Please" or worse, "No Gifts," printed in the lower right-hand corner. (I think *gift* is an unattractive and somewhat cheesy word and I much prefer *present*.) The motives behind this unsettling directive remain obscure (unless your guest list is so extensive that you'd have to take a leave of absence from your job to write thank-you notes). When a hostess has spent days preparing for a party by scraping the mildew off the shower curtain, wrapping up little hot dogs in phyllo dough and baking them, and enlarging embarrassing high school yearbook photographs and stationing them at strategic points around the living room for guests to snicker at for years to come, she deserves a little something. Having birthday parties without presents is like taking away Christmas and replacing it with Flag Day.

Since RSVP stands for *répondez s'il vous plaît,* or respond if you please, it is not necessary to have "Please RSVP" printed on your invitations.

And when you call your hostess to respond to an invitation, do not say, "I'm calling to RSVP," and assume that your hostess thinks that you're accepting. You are responding, but it's up to you to tell her that you're either attending or not. You should be specific and say, "I would love to come to your cocktail party" or "I'm so sorry that I won't be able to come to your cocktail party."

There seems to be a movement afoot to put "Not

Black Tie" on invitations. I trust you will not be a part of it. This is unnecessary, because unless the host or hostess says it is "Black Tie," it's not. Some will say, "I have no choice but to put 'Not Black Tie' on the invitation because otherwise people don't know what to wear and they call me." Let 'em call. It's their problem, not yours.

I think that's as much as I can absorb about invitations. What advice do you have about the actual event?

If you are late for dinner at someone's house, don't bring your hostess a bunch of flowers as a gesture of contrition. Believe me, at that point the last thing she wants to think about is going into the kitchen and finding a vase, filling it, and arranging some flowers. If you want to apologize for your tardiness, send her a plant or flowers, in a vase, the next day. And don't be late again.

Have music playing, especially during the cocktail hour. And turn up the volume a bit more than you would if there were only two of you present. If the volume is higher than usual, but not enough to be piercing or annoying, your guests will have to speak up, thereby making the evening seem more festive and exciting.

If the occasion is a seated lunch or dinner, and you have to rent tables, rent fewer large ones.

Don't invite forty people and seat them at ten tables of four. Use four tables that seat ten guests. Otherwise, the whole notion of talking to many different people is lost. You might as well be playing Scrabble.

Don't even think of asking to sit next to your boyfriend or husband at a dinner party. This is too tiresome for your hostess. Why would you want to sit beside the person you come with? Isn't the purpose of a party to have a spirited conversation with other people, to meet someone who might tell you something that would make you look differently at life, to share a truly riveting piece of gossip with your date on the way home as you rehash the evening? If not, then the two of you should stay at home, order in burritos, and watch *Friends* reruns.

Once I went to a dinner party and sat beside a woman, and my date was sitting next to a man. There were six men and six women. Why did I end up with a woman when there were enough men to go around?

That happened because traditionally the hostess has to be at one head of the table and her husband at the other, but that no longer makes sense. It's not as though you are still a child with your mother and father at opposite ends of the table.

The hostess can sit at one end of the table, closest to the kitchen, and her husband can sit wherever. This way, there will be a woman at the head of the table, but who cares? The seating arrangement will be boy/girl, boy/girl.

When you give a dinner party, do consider inviting one guest who may be more outspoken and opinionated than the others. A party made up of tasteful and well-behaved people can be tedious, but someone whom you can count on to be a bit offensive can really move the evening along. I once overheard a woman say to another guest at a dinner at our house, "You know, I told my husband that you are the bravest woman I know."

"Really," said the other guest, pleased and flattered. "Why is that?"

"Because you had your family Christmas card photographs taken without having your hairdresser do something about your dark roots, and I don't know when I've ever heard of a more courageous act," she said, nodding and smiling. "I've told everyone," she added.

Mommy, that was you with the dark roots!

Yes, and I never invited that woman back. But it did make for a memorable evening. Unless you're giving a small dinner and all are friends anyway, sit your guests next to people they'd like to know, not those with whom they are already well acquainted. And if you're having three couples and one single woman for dinner, place the unescorted woman between two men and seat two of the other women beside each other. Don't penalize the single woman for not bringing a date and at least provide her with one for dinner.

If you are the host of a large dinner party and have several tables, do not give into temptation to put all your least-enchanting guests together and in your mind call it the Alpo table. They'll figure it out and be justifiably cross and hurt. And they *will* figure it out.

Sometimes it's necessary to give a dinner guest whom you really like a tiresome or annoying dinner partner on one side. This is perfectly permissible as long as you make up for it by providing that guest with a charmer on the other side.

Some of my friends say that there are subjects that you can't discuss at dinners or parties. Why do they say that and do you think they're right?

I was chatting away at a dinner party one evening and suddenly my hostess said, "Oh, please, we don't talk about politics or religion at our dinners." I shouldn't have been surprised by her words or her frozen smile. There is a prohibition on discussing sex, politics, and religion on social

occasions, ostensibly because these subjects that
are so near to people's hearts are also too upset-
ting, particularly if the guests argue about them. I
disagree and have never understood the rationale
behind this edict. Even though I am an atheist,
among my most enjoyable and memorable dinner
partners have been a Catholic priest, an Episco-
palian bishop, and a university chaplain. I am
also a liberal Democrat who spends many
evenings with Republicans. A former cabinet
member in a Republican administration once sat
on my right at a dinner table and at one point informed me that I was "the liberal backwash of our
dismal past." But it wasn't said with anger, and
once I determined that *backwash* didn't necessarily apply to my hair, I found the description almost beguiling. Almost.

Personally, I think there's nothing more fun to
talk about and debate than sex, politics, and religion. Since there is more often than not a sex
scandal going on in Washington or Hollywood, it's
hard to avoid it and really, who'd want to? As for
politics, life is politics; it's what we are, and one of
the benefits of living in a democracy is being able
to discuss our elected officials, how they're voting,
and with whom they are sleeping.

Why can't we discuss issues that are close to
our hearts? What is it that intelligent, thinking
adults should talk about? Moisturizing creams

and whose child is showing signs of projectile vomiting? It is possible to discuss potentially controversial issues without attacking people or ignoring their feelings.

If you feel strongly about a political or social issue and it stirs your soul, then talk about it. Argue about it. Maybe you'll change someone's mind or maybe someone will change yours. But don't be afraid to speak up.

And what if I sit next to someone who doesn't want to discuss anything?

Occasionally, you will find yourself at a dinner party, haplessly trying to make conversation with a man who thinks you exist only to draw him out. A man who—after you have inquired about his job, where his children go to school, what he thinks about the latest political scandal, and his favorite vacation spots—asks you nothing about yourself. If you're not asking, they're not talking. A man who, if you had a sudden heart attack and slid off your chair and onto the floor, would never notice. A man who will finally turn to you at the end of the evening and pose the thought-provoking question: "Are you sure this coffee is decaf?" If you just heard the hostess mention to another guest that she ran out of decaf that morning, you have my permission to smile and say, "Oh, yes, it's decaf."

~~~~~~

When I was younger, I thought there was no worse fate than sitting next to a woman at dinner, but after the decaf guy and some of the other men I've encountered, give me a woman any time. They will nod sympathetically when I explain that I remove my contact lenses and my nail polish before I weigh myself. Women are also more likely to initiate a conversation by asking, "Do you know what I hate?" And that's a much more intriguing conversation starter than coffee.

I once sat between two men at a dinner party and began a political discussion with the person on my right. His views were quite extreme, not to say wacko and hateful. He was not the best listener in the world and insisted upon repeating his opinions several times, at a deliberately slow pace, as if I were too slow to comprehend anything said quickly. After twenty minutes of this, I turned to the attractive man on my left, whom I had met just an hour before, and said, "I'm going to shoot myself if I have to talk to my other dinner partner much longer." He answered, "I'd love to help you out but I'm having a few problems myself with the woman on my other side. Sorry." I reluctantly returned to my first partner, attempting to remember the relaxation exercises I had learned years before in a yoga class. Just as I was trying to figure out how to breathe in through my left nostril and out through my right without anyone thinking I was very odd, the man on my left tapped my arm and said, as I turned to him, "Okay, since the woman on my left is no longer speaking to me, I'm all yours." The man on my left more than made up for his counterpart on my right. No matter how unpromising a situation seems at the beginning, it's possible to have a happy and gratifying ending.

My husband is always quick to remind me that not every woman at a dinner party is a combination of Catherine Zeta-Jones and Katie Couric. He once sat beside a beautiful, bright, and chatty woman who informed him during the soup course that she had just completed a course in martial arts that she had taken after being mugged. She then offered that if any man ever so much as touched her again, he'd better take his best shot because she'd kill him in a flash with her new-found skills. Unfortunately, during the course of this exchange, my husband developed a cramp in his leg, which was wedged beneath a rather crowded table. In his attempt to straighten it out and ease the pain, he grew most apprehensive about inadvertently touching his dinner partner's foot. He was certain he'd be dead by dessert.

In spite of the possibility of landing just such a loser for a dinner partner, switching place cards at dinner parties, without your hostess's approval, is tantamount to, if not worse than, grand-theft auto. Placement is the decision of the hostess, not her guests. If you don't like your dinner partners, get over it. Eleven o'clock eventually comes around.

What do you think of a hostess who invites you for dinner and then orders takeout?

If you are giving a big cocktail party, or having more than eight guests for dinner, I would recommend takeout. You don't want to spend all your time in the kitchen, away from your guests, if you can avoid it. Nobody notices or cares where the food originated. The guests and conversation are what people take away and remember from a party, not the food.

I have also learned, from years of parties that I have given and those that I've attended, that the food that people enjoy is straightforward and uncomplicated, like chicken pot pie or meat loaf and mashed potatoes. If you can't afford to order out, give the party with a friend and split the expenses.

The difficult part of being a hostess is folding the napkins, making sure that each guest—even the one you don't particularly like but had to invite anyway—is involved in conversation, and washing the dishes. The gratifying part is that the hostess is in charge and makes all the decisions, including what she serves. If she wants to order take-out food and serve it on her grandmother's china and pretend she made everything from scratch, it's her choice. Dinner parties are not about the honor system.

beauty tips, or where to put the bronzer

~~~~~~

Mommy, my first question is, why do you have hundreds of lipsticks, all in the same color? And what are your other guidelines?

Because it is my steadfast belief that when I have indeed managed to locate the perfect lipstick shade, my hair will look thicker.

Since you asked, my basic beauty rules are the following:

➤ Be aware that low knees can make your legs look short. However, I am convinced that tanned legs make your knees look higher, which will, in turn, make your legs look longer. Be sparing with the self-tanner, though; too much will make them look like Cheetos. (Although if they look long, who cares?)

➤ If you decide to submit to full-body electrolysis, a time-consuming and staggeringly boring process, plan to undergo psychotherapy or take Italian lessons at the same time.

➤ Use Vaseline to hydrate dry lips and to comb your eyebrows and keep them in place.

➤ As you are applying concealer to your face with a small fine-tipped makeup brush, make sure that you put it on the inner and outer corners of your eyes. It will brighten up your whole face.

➤ Use pressed powder with a yellow base to do speedy touch-ups. And the perfect tone for a cream blush is that which most closely resembles your cheek color after a robust workout.

➤ When you sample lipsticks in a store, test them on your fingertips. This gives an accurate sense of how the color will appear on your lips. And it is possible to apply lipstick without a mirror as long as you concentrate on one object. Soldiers in the jungle shave each day by staring at a tree trunk; if they can do it without a mirror, you can, too.

➤ Know that as significant as lipstick is, hair occupies an even more exalted position in my brain (which may be so muddled by years of peroxide that I am no longer fit to make any pronouncements). I've learned that if you leave your house with flat hair and lipstick on your teeth, the odds are 90 to 1 that you will run into a guy who dumped you or the girl for whom he dumped you. Believe me on this one.

➤ Consider one piece of advice that I wish I had learned earlier. When you have your hair cut at the same time you're getting a manicure, after the manicurist applies the polish, make sure your palms are facing up. It is no fun watching slips of hair float down from your head to become embedded in your wet nails.

➤ If your hair is limp, use mousse after shampooing, not a cream conditioner. Conditioners can weigh down skimpy hair that tangles easily, but mousse will allow you to comb it out without snarls and add a little body as well. Also, water that's too hot will dry out your hair.

➤ Do not take the rollers out of your hair while your hair is still hot from the hair dryer or the heated rollers; it must be cool in order for the curl to set.

➤ Do not touch up hair color for at least a month.

➤ Realize that contrary to what my mother always told me, that as long as hair is clean it will look pretty, this is not true. Actually, I find hair that is full of saltwater and beach air is easier to manage than hair that is newly shampooed. And shoulder-length hair is more flattering than really long hair.

➤ Be wary of salespeople at makeup counters. A clerk once informed me that deep lilac eye shadow would make my decidedly brown eyes green. After she had her way with my eyelids, I thought—for one brief, shining moment—that I spotted some minuscule but defiant green specks. I was deeply mistaken. I learned that these salespeople don't always have your best interests or high cheekbones at heart. Really black mascara doesn't make one's eyes any lighter either.

➤ Use a lash primer on your eyelashes before applying mascara; it makes all the difference. Your lashes will indeed look thicker, curlier, and longer. I don't know why it took me so long to come around to this most important beauty product.

➤ Remember that bronzers are important. Nearly everyone looks better with a tan. You can make your face glow by using a bit of shimmer along the cheekbones, the bridge of your nose, and your temples. These are the areas the sun would hit you if you were lying on the beach.

➤ Be careful when you're spraying perfume on yourself; avoid getting any on your jewelry, especially pearls. It dulls them. You can apply it to the inside of your wrists, but that was the custom a century ago when men kissed women's hands. These days, I think it's more effective on your hair and neck. Additionally, don't keep your perfume bottles in a window where the perfume can deteriorate from the sun's rays. For future reference, perfume can also be harmful when it comes into contact with fur coats or fur collars.

➤ Clean out your makeup bag from time to time and toss anything that's more than two years old. And then chuck whatever is broken or that you haven't used in the past six months. In addition, remember that foundation in bottles and loose powder are meant to stay put in your makeup drawer at home, not to go on the road where the bottles will break and the powder will flake.

➤ Go to a professional eyebrow technician and have her tweeze or wax your brows. The closest thing to having plastic surgery without going under the knife is having your eyebrows professionally groomed. Your eyebrows frame your face and a few quick plucks can take you from Frida Kahlo to fabulous. The improvement is immediate and remarkable and well worth the price. If you plan to maintain your brows yourself between appointments, stay away from magnifying mirrors and don't pick up your tweezers every time you look into your makeup mirror. You don't want your frame to become too sparse. When you do tweeze, don't go above your eyebrows; just concentrate on the bone below your brow. If you run out of brow gel and Vaseline, a lip moisture lipstick works just as well at keeping your eyebrows from resembling those of Saddam Hussein. And if you are a blonde or becoming a blonde, you might consider lightening your eyebrows as well, unless you want to look like Madonna on her "Blonde Ambition" tour.

3

fashion advice, or no tank tops at the ritz

and one more thing . . .

Before we get too deeply involved in your style rules, I have to ask you something really important. Is there really a way of telling a real Prada bag, or any designer handbag, from a knockoff?

With Prada bags, the difference is in the zipper and the leather piece on the zipper. Since this is a rather obscure bit of knowledge, I say, go with the fake. Of course, it would be worth your while to know the specific models of the real deals since some copies are made in a style that Prada has never produced. Moreover, in a legitimate bag, the logo will never be cut off at any seam, but the copies have no such compunction and will often slash right through the logo. The linings of the fake bags are sometimes different from the genuine articles. For example, a faux bag may be lined with a completely different fabric from what is used with the real thing. The lining of the knockoff Louis Vuitton bags are often nicer and softer than real LV bags, which have no lining at all. Go figure.

What about fake jewelry? If someone compliments me on it, should I pretend that it's real?

Only if you hate the person who's admiring it. I always tell my real friends the truth about the fakes.

Why do you get cranky when I ask to borrow something of yours? You should be flattered that I find any of your clothes wearable.

When you have a daughter who borrows your clothes, and who, when asked for the thirteenth time to return them, says earnestly, "But I put them back, Mommy. They're in your 'loser' closet," you may begin to understand a mother's reluctance to make additional loans. And the closet that you think is for my loser clothes is actually for the clothes I'm not wearing that particular season, Missy.

Not that you asked my advice, but shoes, belts, and handbags have a contrived, assembled look when they match. If your belt and shoes are the same color, that is sufficient. Furthermore, if you're wearing a pale blue shirt or pants, camel or brown-toned shoes and belt look better than black.

Why do you tie your sweaters around various parts of your body, rather than actually wear them?

A sweater knotted casually around the neck never goes out of style and can camouflage many imperfections, such as annoyingly narrow shoulders, a skimpy ponytail, or a missing button on your blouse. You can also tie a sweater around your middle to conceal a less than sleek waistline and hips. Or pants that don't fit. Tying a sweater around your shoulders is an art, not a science, but here's what I've learned. If it's a cardigan, make sure it's buttoned, then fold it over at the sleeves and toss it over your shoulders with the buttons facing in. Tie it once or twice. Europeans are far more adept at this fashion than we are.

Do you have a problem with T-shirts? You do seem to mention them a lot.

I'm quite fond of T-shirts as long as they don't come with slogans printed on them. Nobody really cares where you've been, which is all too often either a hot dog–eating contest in Atlantic City or the "It's a Small World After All" or "Mad Tea Party" ride at Walt Disney World.

What would you consider fashion essentials, without spending a lot of money?

You should build your winter wardrobe around a black pantsuit and a basic wool or tweed jacket that you can wear over everything. For example, you can wear the jacket with a white shirt and a camel-colored bag and sweater.

For spring, a lightweight wool or cotton blazer

in navy will see you through most occasions. It will look equally chic with navy, khaki, or white pants. Dark brown shoes, rather than black, look better with navy pants or skirts. Beige, yellow, and light blue tops also work well with navy.

Must-haves also include the essential black cocktail dress, a pair of perfectly fitting jeans, a black turtleneck, one pair of great boots, and one pair of classic black closed-toed heels. The discomfort of the shoes is almost worth it for the wonders they perform for your legs.

And what are those rules again about seasonal dressing? When can I wear what and what about colors? Furthermore, what are your other fashionista guiding principles? Or in some cases, commands?

➤ Do not wear linen before Memorial Day or after Labor Day. No velvet before November or after February and no ultrasuede in any season. It is now acceptable to wear white during the winter months, but I can think of no reason *ever* to own any article of clothing in maroon or mustard shades.

➤ When you're wearing capri pants, make sure your shoes are either flat or have only tiny heels. And for narrow pants, wear only flats or short boots. Higher heeled shoes should be worn only with straight or full pants. Wearing high heels with capri pants is not a fashion approach that you should embrace, unless you fancy looking like the Pink Ladies in the movie *Grease*. And when you're using the word *Capri* to describe the island, the accent is on the first syllable ('Ca-pri); when you're talking about the pants, the accent is on the second (ca-'pri).

➤ If you're wearing a turtleneck, lose the pearls and chains and just wear a pin or clip. (Unless you want to look the way your mother did in 1974.)

➤ Use your Hermès scarf, or any favorite kerchief, as a bikini top. Don't tie it around the handle of your bag. (Unless you want to look the way your grandmother did in 1974.)

➤ Make sure that the sleeves of your shirts, jackets, and coats are not so long that they touch the top of your hand. To remedy this and other vexing details, use a tailor. They're not expensive and they can create the most minor alterations that make a significant difference in your clothes and how they fit. They can also make subtle revisions in last year's wardrobe that will be satisfyingly up-to-date and no one will guess that what you're wearing today wasn't bought yesterday. Your tailor should be as important as your hair colorist or your aesthetician. Having a jacket or dress fitted properly will make the same understated but worthwhile improvement in your appearance that properly tended eyebrows do to your face.

➤ Remember, there is a little black dress for every season; only the fabric changes. However, a little navy blue dress is a softer color and more appealing for the summer months.

➤ When in doubt, send your clothes to the dry cleaners.

Do all these rules constitute some basic fashion philosophy that I should live by?

What I'm about to tell you falls far short of a philosophy, even for me, but this is what I've come up with. You may think that you have a style of dressing that is fairly entrenched, only to find that you're entirely influenced by location and culture and are without a personal signature when it comes to fashion.

For instance, if I go to Italy in the summer, I begin my vacation dressed as an American: white T-shirt, khaki shorts, brown sandals, small pearl stud earrings, and very little makeup. By day three on the Italian Coast, I am wearing a blue linen shirt, yellow pants, white sandals, gold dan-

gly earrings, and bright lipstick. And here's the
rub: Even though I look better in Italy than I do at
home, by the time I return to these shores, I'm
back in tacky khaki and boring pearl studs.

I don't want to dwell too much on Italian style,
although I do think it's the best, but many wear
blue shirts with red pants and it looks really good.

It's so easy to know when you've got Italy on your
mind. You wear the collars of your jackets and
shirts turned up.

Yes, and perfect strangers come up to me on the
street and turn them down again. There's something about this look that I'm missing.

Would your clothing tips for "When I go to Italy
in the summer" also apply to a three-bedroom
summer share house with twenty other renters, as
well as an evening that includes Blockbuster
Video at the local mall? And why do you change
what you wear when you "return to these shores"?

What's cool on Capri doesn't always work on Cape
Cod. But if you look as attractive as you can, you'll
receive extra consideration at job and school inter-
views and better tables in restaurants. And even
at Blockbuster, you'll get your DVDs faster.

Once when I was visiting a college roommate on Cape Cod and I wrapped a sarong around my bathing suit to go to the beach, she looked at me and said, "We don't wear those wrap-around things here." I didn't know what to say.

Maybe it was her first year there. Be more resolute than she was or I am. I always think you should wear what suits your figure and your own sense of style and ease. However, I wouldn't suggest that you go topless on Nantucket.

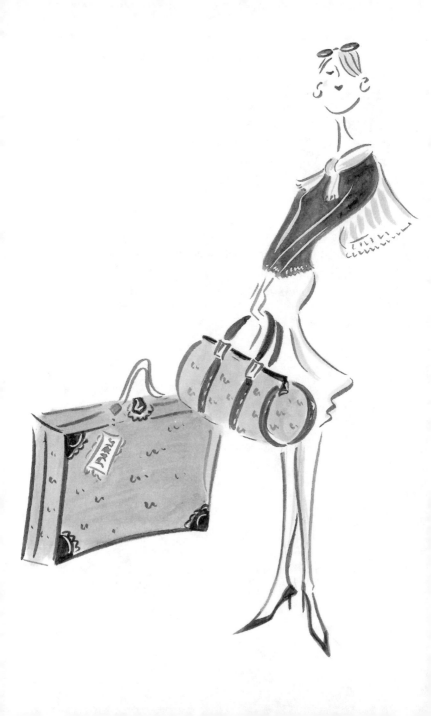

4

traveling large and packing light

and one more thing . . .

When I was a little girl and we were traveling, why did you always make me dress up as if I were going to a party, when everyone else was wearing nylon sweat suits?

Reread chapter 3. It's also important to dress well when you travel by plane. Aside from the not insignificant fact that you're representing your country when you fly abroad, I acknowledge an old-fashioned but true belief that there's also a much greater possibility of being upgraded to Business or First Class if you're well dressed and look the part. When you are wearing turquoise sweatpants and a pink baseball cap bearing the message "Getting Lucky in Kentucky" you will never sit anywhere but near the bathrooms at the rear of the plane. (On the other hand, if you do stroll through First Class and notice a couple wearing acid-washed jeans and flip-flops, you'll know—without a doubt—that they paid full price.) On a plane, also avoid sitting next to any man wearing a tank top. Actually, avoid men in tank tops at all times, unless you're at a Celtics game.

And once I reach my destination? What is this concierge business you're always talking about?

Once when your father and I arrived at a hotel in Paris, I was in desperate need of a pregnancy test and a hairdresser. I really had no choice about my hair. We were having dinner with his former girlfriend (or wife, I can't always be sure with him), and I had to look my best. As for being pregnant, I was pretty sure I was, but of course, I wanted to be certain. Because I had tipped the concierge *immediately upon my arrival,* within minutes of my asking, he produced Docteur Boisvert and his pregnancy test and Monsieur Alexandre and his blow-dryer. By the end of the day, I learned that I was indeed pregnant with you, and my hair never looked better. Of course, you would have been born anyway, and the only guarantee of my hair looking that good every day would be if I had divorced your father and married Monsieur Alexandre.

The concierge will help you with theater tickets, restaurant reservations, and travel to and from the airport, so hand over a tip from twenty-five to fifty dollars when he or she makes your first reservation. This way, you will be remembered and given special attention. Do not ask for help and then wait until the day you leave to give a tip. You want the concierge working his little heart out *during* your stay, not just his warm thanks at the end.

Why does every story go back to your hair?

Just let me finish, and stop rolling your eyes. If the first hotel room you are shown is not to your liking, do ask to see another in the same price range. Hotels try to get rid of their less desirable rooms and they will show whatever the traffic or traveler will bear.

Now, I understand that you may not always be staying in big hotels and many people like nothing better than staying at bed-and-breakfast inns while they travel, but believe me, you pay a lot of money for no television, telephone, closet, or room service. Staying at a B&B is not unlike staying at the house of someone you know. And hate.

What about packing? What should I always take on a trip?

In terms of clothes, you won't have to cart as much if you pack pants and skirts in navy or black and (depending on the season) khaki, beige, and white. Take along jackets and tops in those same shades. You can bring sweaters in brighter, more interesting hues. But, generally, organize your travel wardrobe around one or two basic colors. If you leave for a trip with a suitcase that's only three-quarters full, you have more room for the clothes you might buy on the road.

Aside from clothes, which I covered previously, I think that the five traveling essentials are a small blow-dryer, cuticle clippers, Band-Aids, cell phone charger, and lots of paperback books. A dryer from home is of the greatest importance because many of those attached to bathroom walls in hotels are so weak that a two-week-old baby could yawn on your hair and dry it faster. Make certain that you have the proper electricity converter if you're going out of the country. The cuticle clippers are so important, and not just for that tiresome hangnail. After you shop, you'll need some way of cutting the tags off your new clothes, particularly if you decide to wear them that night. And if you're in Athens and have blisters on your feet from climbing up and down the Parthenon, it will save many trips to the pharmacy if your Band-Aids are right alongside an extra shower cap in your makeup bag.

If your cell phone dies in the middle of a trip, you'll have to use the hotel phone, which will be much more expensive than your cell. I think you'd prefer to use your traveling funds for shopping rather than your phone bill.

When you're traveling abroad, pack more than enough paperbacks to see you through your trip. There's nothing more pitiful—after learning that the bookstore in town carries only Books on Tape in Urdu—than being forced to chat up and buy drinks for other American tourists, hoping they'll leave you a book or two. Finding yourself stuck in a hotel room, wanting only to lose yourself in a good novel, is worse luck still when the books tossed your way by your fellow travelers are *The New Age Astral Guide* and *Cooking Your Way to Thin Ankles*.

Should you ever happen to outgrow duffel bags and decide to use suitcases, pack your shirts and dresses on the same thin white wire hangers that dry cleaners use when they hand you your newly cleaned and pressed clothes. Put your pants and skirts on pant hangers. Packing this way will take up a tiny bit more space, but unpacking and repacking will be wondrously and speedily improved because they're never off the hangers and they go directly from your suitcase to the closet and back.

And when I return from any foreign trip?

When you arrive at Customs, don't even think of not declaring items that you have to pay duty on, unless you think it's worth going to jail to save one hundred and fifty dollars for two pantsuits that you bought in London that were on sale anyway. Once, upon returning from Europe, I declared a gold bracelet on my customs form. When the customs inspector asked if he could see the piece of jewelry in question, I proudly stuck out my arm and showed it to him, in all its gleaming glory. I was shocked to see the expression on his face, which shifted from bafflement to disdain.

I said, "You hate it."

He looked at the store receipt, then back to my bracelet, shook his head slightly and said, "I'm not saying a thing."

"You can't believe I paid that much money for it, can you?" I asked, trying not to whimper.

"Lady," he said, "it's none of my business. As long as you like it, fine." Then he looked at the receipt once more and rolled his eyes, just slightly, but I saw it.

I'd have been happier in jail.

You know, when I go anywhere, just on my own or with friends, traveling seems to be such a hassle that I can't imagine doing it with children.

It is, but when you have young children and are actually planning and taking trips, it's not the daunting process it becomes as you grow older and look back.

If you're traveling with a baby, consider taking not only a change of clothes for your child, but also for yourself. A friend was once on a plane with a woman whose baby had spit up all over herself and her mother. The baby had a lovely change of clothes but the mother had nothing to change into from her black linen jacket that had taken on a rather unattractive mottled quality. Also, when traveling with young children, a mother can't bring along too many ziplock bags. For every-thing.

And don't spend too much time in Washington, D.C., with children. After being there once for three days, your then eight-year-old brother looked at me closely and said, "Mommy, with that shirt on, you look like James Knox Polk."

Very young children can make traveling easier, at least at the beginning of your trip. People flying with babies and toddlers can go to the head of the passenger line, in front of those less fortunate travelers whose children are all now teenagers. If you're careful, and space your progeny properly, you can arrange early boarding for a good part of your life. And when they do become sullen teenagers, at least they can help with the luggage.

5

food, shelter, and the pottery barn

(and other pesky details, now that you're living on your own)

your apartment

What is your advice for girls who are moving away from their parents' house and into their own apartment or house?

Oh, do you mean now that they have to deal with everything that their mothers took care of in the past?

First of all, when you move into a new apartment or house, make sure you have the locks changed and leave an extra key with a family member or good friend. If you have moved to an apartment, alone or with a roommate, tip the building superintendent about fifty dollars before or as soon as you get settled and say, "I'll probably need you in the future and I will be grateful for your help." And also tip him, and your doormen, if you have any, at Christmas. If you're not certain how much to give them, ask other tenants in the building. If you can manage it, I think thirty to fifty dollars for the super and twenty dollars for the elevator men and/or doormen will suffice. When your pipes burst in the middle of the night, it's comforting to know that because you have a well-tipped and appreciative super who will come to your aid, you won't have to sleep on a life preserver and have all your strappy stilettos ruined in the flood.

If you're living in a city and your apartment doesn't have a doorman, ask the cab driver who brings you home at night to wait until you're safely inside the front door before he drives off. Not having a doorman also means you can't get deliveries when you are away from home, but if you're pleasant and friendly to the people who work in nearby stores, they will often accept packages for you. (And when you do use a delivery man, remember to tip him.) Having a doorman signifies a bit pricier apartment, but it also means you have added security and someone who can zip up your out-of-reach zipper when your roommates aren't home.

If you and/or your roommate can afford it, a cleaning lady every other week, if only for two hours, is well worth the expense. Make sure the kitchen and bathrooms are spotlessly clean, change your sheets every week, and flip your mattress (and with any luck, not your roommate) once a year.

If you have any remaining money and you feel that your inability to throw away old or never-worn clothes, papers, and old letters is leading to total disorder in your closet, dresser, and desk, I think it would be worth your while and your checkbook to hire a professional organizer just to get everything straightened out. It's a bit like hiring a professional trainer. Once you learn the basics, you should be able to handle the maintenance yourself. I would give up all other expenses except my hair highlighting appointments for this.

Remember to cancel your newspapers when you go on vacation. The neighbors down the hall will not look kindly upon you or a heap of newspapers piled in front of your door for a week.

Is there anything I should always have on hand?

You have no idea of how little I know (or care) about this topic, but I think a flashlight is a necessity—not just for blackouts, but so you can distinguish between your navy blue and black pants at the back of your closet. You have to own two screwdrivers: a Phillips head and a regular. When you see them together, you'll understand why you need both. It's too long and boring an explanation for me to explain further. Buying a plunger ought to round out your essential tool kit.

What about furniture? Where should I buy it?

Go to Ikea or Pottery Barn. There is so much attractive and inexpensive furniture around these days, far more than when I moved into my first apartment and could only afford orange canvas director's chairs and shag rugs that looked used even when they were new.

and one more thing . . .

~~~~~~~~~~~~~~~~~~~~~~~~~~~~~~

What is the deal on thread counts and sheets?

I have no idea what it means. Something about the higher the thread count, the finer the sheets. If you buy sheets by a brand or company you've heard of, they will probably do nicely. It's as difficult for me to figure out thread counts (which sound oddly similar to *threadbare*) as it is when people tell me the number of square feet in their houses or apartments. It means nothing to me because I can't picture the size of rooms according to the square feet. Or the crispness or softness of pillowcases according to the count.

What should I do about telephone solicitors?

Answer the phone and say, "I do not take solicitations over the phone but you may contact me by mail. Good-bye." This way, you're not being rude to some hardy soul whose days are spent listening to people yell at or hang up on him. But you don't have to give up dinner, either.

What about roommates?

I think that ideally, you should have one, maybe two. But if four or five of you share an apartment, it's going to feel as if you are back in a college dorm and you will lose some of the sense of living on your own. And of course, the living will be much easier if there is financial equality among or between your apartment mates. If the two girls (or boys) making less money have to share a bedroom while you live in solitary splendor in the single room, or vice-versa, it could get tense. If you and your roommate aren't getting along, being in a small apartment will only worsen your situation. A friend once told me that her roommate was so angry about being fired from her job that she refused to help out with the housework, except for grudgingly lifting her feet off the floor as my friend vacuumed. I had a college friend whom I thought would be fun to room with after graduation until she informed me that her pet snake had just died on top of her radiator when the dorm turned up the heat.

Do you think I might begin watching too much television, living on my own?

As long as you read the newspaper every day and watch the news, you're free to do whatever you want. And when the Sunday paper arrives, the wedding section does not count as real news. Read the front page as well. Actually, I would worry more if you had no television at all because that would mean you are isolated from what is going on in the world; that's a pretty dangerous position to be in these days.

Of course, it is important to read books. Whether they're novels or mysteries or movie star biographies, just read.

I would also hope, for your sake and the sake of those around you, particularly those who aren't as young and fortunate as you and your friends, that you would do some kind of community service or volunteer work. It will make *you* feel better, believe me. And then you can really watch television to your heart's content.

Do I have to call you all the time?

Not all the time, but I would like to stay in touch. I think that in this age of cell phones and e-mail, more communication is expected from girls by their mothers than was the case when women of my generation were starting out. We would call our mothers once a week, collect if we could, and write the very occasional postcard if we lived in a different city. But expectations are higher now and it's not that difficult to send off an e-mail or call your parents. And it will keep them calm and contented and you can go about your life. E-mail is a less emotional way of staying connected. You can't be driven crazy by a hint of sadness in your mother's voice that she might toss into the conversation because she's lonesome for you—because you can't hear it in an e-mail and she won't write it. (Well, she might, but you'll have the chance to think of a reason why you won't be coming to dinner before you reply.)

kitchen clues

All I can remember of your kitchen advice is to cook the bacon slowly. I don't do much cooking. None of my friends do, either.

Yes, I noticed that your morning coffee is takeout from the diner across the street. If I weren't your mother, I might think that you'd been raised by wolves.

The reality is that people just don't cook as often as they used to. When girls live alone, they're much more likely to pick up something for dinner on the way home from work. People also work long hours and don't have time to cook when they get home at night.

If you have time to cook and you enjoy it, that's terrific. And even if you order out a lot, you should still have a few dinner selections under your belt. Cooking is not difficult. If you can read a recipe in a cookbook, you can cook. And if you can read a menu and own a microwave, you can order in. In the meantime, I'm going to suggest two possible menus for guests. Or for yourself.

If you're having two or three friends over for dinner, you can have baked potatoes, lamb chops, asparagus, and chocolate cake for dessert. Scrub the potatoes and bake them in the oven at 450 degrees Fahrenheit for an hour. Wash the raw asparagus and bend the stalks until they break, then throw the ends away and place the stalks with tips into a frying pan of boiling water. Turn the burner down until the water is simmering (an understated, quiet boil) and continue cooking from five to ten minutes or until they're tender but not too soft and floppy. While the asparagus is cooking and the potatoes are baking, sauté or fry the lamb chops—two per person unless the chops are very thin, and then plan on three—in a frying pan, which you have already prepared with melted butter or extra-virgin olive oil. Fry the chops until they're brown and then cook them over a low heat and check them for doneness with a knife from time to time. Most people enjoy eating them when they're crispy on the outside and pale pink on the inside.

That's easy for you to say. It's the timing that's tricky.

That gets easier with experience. The more practice you have in the kitchen, the more you'll understand how much time is required for each dish. This whole dinner will take an hour, but only the last fifteen minutes require the same amount of attention that you give to deep-conditioning your hair. Buy a jar of mint jelly to serve alongside the lamb chops, and offer butter for the potatoes and asparagus.

Roasting a chicken is also easy; the actual preparation is about ten minutes and the cooking takes only a few hours. The instructions are written on the plastic that the chicken comes wrapped in, so it's hard to misplace them. Before I cook a chicken (and after washing it in the kitchen sink and drying it with paper towels) I brush olive oil or butter on the breast and legs, sprinkle kosher salt and pepper over it, and stuff it with either a peeled onion or a whole lemon (I poke holes in the lemon so the flavor seeps out). Cook it at 350 degrees Fahrenheit uncovered for an hour. You can serve this with mashed potatoes (boil potatoes, then pierce them with a fork to steam before you mash them with warmed milk and butter) and frozen peas that take four minutes to heat in the microwave.

Buy a chocolate cake and serve it with freshly washed raspberries and mint leaves. This is not arduous but your guests will think you have great culinary skills; they'll never suspect that this is all you can cook. Once you learn the rudiments of the kitchen, you can explore new recipes.

Or go back to the diner across the street?

Or buy a cookbook. I know it's a bit early for you to give some thought to this subject, but there is a fundamental reason for you to have some family recipes on hand. When your future children come home from college, you can fix their favorite dinner, the one they've been longing for and talking about ever since leaving home. And believe me, it will not be takeout from Big Nick's Leaning Tower of Pizza.

your bank account

(make sure <u>you</u> can do the math)

and one more thing . . .

Even though finances are so far removed from your area of experience or knowledge, is there <u>anything</u> you can tell me?

I know less about money and managing it than I do about thread counts and I am sorry that I didn't learn more about it when I was your age. It would have been helpful. Don't make this mistake. My husbands have been in charge of this aspect of my life, which is a good thing, because without them, I'd probably be homeless.

Men always took care of you. Why shouldn't that happen to me?

Because it's the twenty-first century and I want you to be financially independent and in charge of your own life. To do that, you've got to have some knowledge of money, how to earn it, and what to do with it once you've got it.

Young women should marry because they're madly in love, not because they can't pay the rent or buy a car. And if a woman turns thirty-five or forty with no prospective husband in sight and chooses to have a baby without being married, she should have the financial resources to raise that child by herself. It's her decision and in many instances, it's the right one.

Most of us have come a long way, baby, and

you should be as knowledgeable about your finances as you are about your lip liners. I've asked people who know more about this than I do, which is just about anyone, and I've learned the following:

➤ Do not spend all your money on Prada sweaters and Manolo Blahnik shoes. While you're young and have a flat tummy and firm thighs, it's not necessary to use up vats of money on clothes. Save your clothing money for the future when you're the mother of a college student yourself and have more cellulite and have a less-than-taut tummy and your figure requires more expensive and forgiving duds. (And, believe me, the men in your life right now don't care what you wear. Expensive clothes will be lost on them.)

➤ Get a credit card immediately and pay the balance off promptly each month. This will build up your credit rating and is extremely important, especially if you ever try to buy a house or an apartment.

➤ Don't think that when you receive your tax refund, the money is a present from the government and you deserve to buy a new iPod with it; it is *your* money you're getting back. You haven't won a lottery. Use it and any year-end bonuses to pay off your credit card debt or invest it.

➢ If the company you work for has a 401(k) or an IRA (individual retirement account), start putting money into it immediately. If you leave the company for another, you can roll over your 401(k) plan. This means it's portable and you can take it to your next employer's 401(k).

➢ Whenever possible, save money by tagging along on family vacations.

➢ Don't invest in the stock market unless you're close to being debt-free. If you do buy stocks and if the value of the stock declines more than 20 percent, realize that you have made an error and sell it.

➢ Remember that economic knowledge will give you power and independence. Use it.

Is it true that you should never lend money to friends? What if they're in real trouble?

I think if a friend truly needs money and you have it, you should lend it. But if you do, accept the fact that when someone owes you money, the relationship between the borrower and the lender is altered, sometimes permanently. The loan is rarely repaid in a timely fashion and when it isn't, it's difficult to ask for it back. Furthermore, the money may be spent in ways that you don't approve of but over which you have no control.

I once loaned money to a childhood friend who wished to have her thighs revised by liposuction. Evidently, when the surgery was completed, she had a little cash left, which she promptly used for a spa weekend in San Diego. I recovered from my disappointment with her decision, but I think of this episode when I see people offering a dollar bill to a homeless person, shaking their fingers, and admonishing, "I'll give you this money, but I hope you'll spend it wisely." Whatever the recipient chooses to do with the cash is his decision, and if you're going to make a contribution, just do it with a smile, skip the lecture, and move on.

If you lend money to a friend and are not paid back, the situation ultimately interferes with the relationship as the lender becomes a critic of the borrower's lifestyle. And that's no way to run a friendship.

Yikes. That's more than you had to say about traveling with children. Are there any rules about investing in real estate? I mean when I have some money?

A very shrewd man once said, "Artists make real estate." If you follow the migration of artists from

the Left Bank of Paris to Provincetown, Massa-
chusetts, and from Manhattan's Greenwich Village and Soho to East Hampton on Long Island
and now to Brooklyn, you will see that wherever
they buy or rent, prices rise. It's almost impossible
to go wrong buying property in those areas. Follow the artists and try to buy some real estate,
even if it's a tiny house or small apartment. Those
regions and neighborhoods will become desirable
and important simply because of the people who
move into them. So even if you marry a starving
artist, the future does hold some promise. If you
live long enough.

decorating with more
style than money

Do you have any ideas that don't involve lots of money, but that I can use now that I'm getting married and also have a job that pays enough for curtains?

Frankly, I never had curtains or children (except for my son) until I married. They each seemed too much for me to handle on my own. In the end, though, children were easier.

Here are eleven decorating guidelines that I have used over the years. If you need more, read *Architectural Digest* or hire a professional.

➤ If you have only shades at your windows, keep them completely up or completely down. It is visually unnerving to see them at the halfway mark. Either have a totally open window that provides a view of the outdoors, or pull the shade down, eliminate the view entirely, and be cozy.

➤ If you move into an apartment building, check the size of the freight elevator to make sure it can accommodate large pieces of furniture. Also measure the width and height of your doors. Storage facilities are filled with sofas that wouldn't fit into the elevator or through the front door. And if you're buying a new sofa, measure it before you put any money down.

and one more thing . . .

➤ Make certain that when you place the pillows on your couch, they are not standing on their corners. It looks calculated and dopey.

➤ Abstain from the kitty-corner concept whenever possible. If you have a stack of books or an oblong box, don't place them diagonally on the coffee table. Just set them down squarely, the corner of the book fitting into the corner of the table, where they belong. I think the kitty-corner school of design is not too far removed from the curled pinkie finger on the hand holding the tea cup. Actually, a distant relative of mine, who is the only person I know capable of decorating an entire house using only turquoise and gold as her color scheme, is quite fond of this look.

➤ Light candles (and blow out the flame if you're not going to use them immediately) before placing them in candlesticks. My mother always maintained this, and of course she was right. Unused white wicks on candles look like props, as though the candles were still in the store. If you have a nonworking fireplace, you can light three candles and place them in low, unobtrusive holders on the hearth.

➤ Place your television in the living room, where there is usually the best space, the best light, and the prettiest furniture (and where you should be spending most of your time). People put their televisions in small, dark rooms and then hole up there for the evening. Seems dumb and a great waste. What are you saving the living room for? A cocktail party for the European ambassadors to the United Nations or Tom Cruise, in case he stops by?

➢ Use room lighting wisely. You'll be happier (and your mother will look so much better when she comes to visit) in a room that's under lit rather than over lit. To this end, if you have a lamp with two bulbs, use a pink bulb with a white one. It will cast the most flattering light on you and your guests.

➢ Be aware that bare walls beat out bad art.

➢ On your living room coffee table, create some interest with a combination of books, candlesticks, and flowers. And change the objects around every few months or so. It will make it more interesting for you and your guests.

➢ Use large pieces of furniture in big rooms and keep the slighter, more delicate pieces for those smaller rooms. This scale plays a significant role in decorating.

➢ When you arrange flowers in a vase, use an odd number. Three or five or nine stems appeal to the eye far more than an even number. When a person looks at an even number of flowers (or other objects), the mind's eye divides them into two symmetrical sections. With an uneven bunch of flowers, this cannot be done. I don't know why this is true, any more than I understand why fat men are good dancers, but it is.

8

careers and how to try to have it all

and one more thing . . .

➢ When in doubt about what to wear, take the more conservative approach. And even if you're an unpaid intern, lose the flip-flops for work.

➢ Check your résumé for typos and have a friend double-check it. You'd be amazed at the number of qualified candidates who get turned away at the door because of mistakes in their résumés. Aside from your interview, this is one subject that tells people who you are, but if the résumé is poorly written, you won't make it to the interview. If I were in charge of hiring someone to work for me who was both intelligent and conscientious, bad grammar and random typos on her CV (curriculum vitae) would not sound a promising note.

➢ If asked whether you can do something, say yes and *then* learn how to do it.

➢ If you go shopping on your lunch hour, have the store hold your purchases and pick them up after work. It just doesn't send the right message when your coworkers or boss see you weighted down by shopping bags.

➢ Do your homework before your job interview. As you sit in the human resources department at Estée Lauder, it's not a good idea to be seen applying Revlon lip gloss. Don't take out your Panasonic PDA at your Sony interview.

➤ Believe it nor not, many women are so relieved that they've actually found a job that they're afraid to negotiate for the salary they want. I don't know why women can negotiate the price of a pair of sling-back shoes, but when it comes to their professional careers, they're faint-hearted. If you don't know how to carry out the negotiation discussions, find someone who will help you.

➤ Find out whether your company sponsors continuing education. If you're given the choice between a financed M.B.A. or an extra thousand dollars a year in your salary, choose the M.B.A. It will be more rewarding, both financially and intellectually.

➤ Once you land a job, play by the rules. When you file an expense account after a trip, don't tack on personal massages and the videos you rented in your hotel room. Those are not legitimate business expenditures.

➤ If, after a period of time, you feel you deserve a raise, ask for it. Instead of sitting in silence, hoping someone else will realize how deserving you are, speak up and be your own advocate.

This is your life and no one is going to live it for you, so take charge.

➤ When you receive a promotion, do not talk about it with any of your colleagues until it has been announced publicly. This can lead to jealousy and resentment among your fellow workers. Just tell your parents.

What about all these rules on sexual harassment in the workplace? Remember when my friend Clara and her boss fell in love and had an affair? Everyone went crazy and she finally had to quit her job. What do you think?

I think that I'm happy to be working at home. I know that some of the rules to prevent sexual harassment were urgently needed. But on the other hand, I think it would be troublesome to labor in an office or a used car lot or any place where your superior was forbidden to flirt, have an affair, or fall in love with you. Doesn't sound like much fun to me.

I want to be at home with my children when I have them, but I also want to have a career. I loved having you there when I got home from school every day, and I wouldn't want to deny that to my children. How am I going to make this work?

A happy mother has happy children. If you're satisfied and challenged by whatever it is that you choose to do—stay at home or have a career as well as children—then you will have contented children. When you were born most women stayed at home, so I wasn't faced with the decisions that many families have to make today. Truthfully, although I don't regret one minute of being at home when you were young, if I were your age again, I would probably work outside the house when I had children. By the time your brother was born, eleven years later, most of the women had left the playground for the workplace.

At this point in my life, the actual reason for me to have a career was to be able to truthfully answer the question, asked by everyone from the pediatrician's nurse to other mothers, "What is your daytime number?" I hated that question. My eyes darted furtively as I mumbled, "Gosh, I work so hard and so late and there's all that travel. I'll give you this one number and you can *try* me there whenever you need me." Of course, if I had told the truth, everyone would have known my dirty little secret: I didn't have a job. I stayed at home with my children. I may be one of the few women in the world who needed a job, not only for money or emotional satisfaction, but for a daytime telephone number so that Dr. Solomon's secretary wouldn't think less of me.

The worst time in my nonworking life occurred the year when both of you were applying to schools at the same time: one to college and the other to first grade. (Let that be a lesson to you about allowing your family planning to get out of hand. When your children are eleven years apart in age, one of them is always awake.) I had to fill in the sections of the applications that asked for the mother's profession. I would have lied in a minute. But since parents didn't completely fill out the applications, I lost my opportunity. At that time, fortunately, your brother could read nothing but dinosaur names in their Latin form. Still, I was fearful that if I rigged my answer on his application, casually dropping the fact that I was a vice president at Merrill Lynch, I might be asked to speak on "sucker rallies" and the "inverted yield curve" at Career Day.

When I was the class mother for your class as well as your brother's, I spent many hours calling the other mothers and asking them to walk in the afternoon safety patrol or to help out at the Paperback Book Fair. The mothers who worked were as available and helpful as those who stayed at home, sometimes even more so. (No working mother ever turned me down for the volunteer safety patrol duty or to make brownies for the second-grade bake sale, but I do remember one at-home mother who was unable to even come to the phone because she was having a massage.) It's my opinion that if you're essentially a good, strong, and loving mother, your children will thrive, whether you're at home or at work.

So do whatever pleases you, and if you hear the siren call of the workplace, buff up your briefcase and head out the door. However, I do have two pieces of advice for you. Never cross the office floor without a piece of paper in your hand. It can be a printout of an e-mail from a friend or a paycheck, just as long as it makes you look busy. There. Now you don't have to go to Harvard Business School.

And remember. Don't go all highfalutin on the mothers who stay at home. Just because they don't have a daytime number doesn't mean they're not a part of your world.

9

health

(and lose the cigarettes now)

and one more thing . . .

A few years ago, a guy I was seeing called me at work and as we were talking, he asked me what I did when I wasn't at the office. I said, "Oh, I put on my jogging pants and sneakers, grab a bottle of Evian water, and go for a four-mile run." Everyone I worked with just looked at me and said, "Yeah, right. You are the biggest liar." But if I'd told him the truth, "I go home, drink a six-pack of Diet Coke, smoke fifteen Marlboro Lights, and watch <u>Trauma: Life in the ER</u> on the Discovery Channel," he'd never have called me again.

> And rightly so. I am so happy that you've cleaned up your act. Except for the Diet Coke and *Trauma: Life in the ER.*

Yes, you're always telling me not to smoke and how bad it is for me, but you used to smoke all the time. I've even seen a photograph of you smoking while you nursed me.

> Well, obviously, in those days, everybody smoked cigarettes under conditions that seem appalling to us now, but we didn't realize how treacherous and stupid smoking was. The only people I'm aware of who still smoke are either high school and college kids, tourists visiting from southern Europe, or lost-looking souls pushing around grocery carts

that are filled with empty beer cans and Styro-foam pretzels.

And cigarettes make your teeth less than white, your breath less than appealing, and when you get older, your skin less than unwrinkled. To say nothing of your lungs and heart.

Excuse me? Let's go back for a minute. So you admit that you smoked while you were breast-feeding me?

I was careful. I thought that as long as I didn't get ashes in your hair, everything would be all right. While I nursed you on my right side, I held my cigarette in my left hand.

Actually, I don't know who fared worse under my breast-feeding regime. One day when Nicholas was a baby, I dashed home from having my hair highlighted at the beauty shop, grabbed him, and began nursing. It was only minutes later that I looked down and noticed small globs of hair bleach that had escaped my hair colorist's towel and had rolled down inside my nursing bra to my breast. Having no idea whether my tiny baby had swallowed any, I leaped up, pulled him away from my breast, and looked in his mouth. I didn't see any signs of peroxide, but I assumed that was because he'd eaten it all. I watched him carefully for years. He seems fine but sometimes, when I recall my nursing days, it's a wonder either of my children can read.

When do you think people should see a psychiatrist or therapist or social worker?

If the notion or possibility of seeing someone in the mental health field crosses your mind more than twice, it's probably a good idea and worth exploring. There's no point in suffering from anxiety or depression when you could be helped.

How would you go about finding someone to see?

Ask your internist, gynecologist, or family doctor.

Fortunately my biggest health problem right now is not being able to fall asleep at night.

If you're lying in bed and can't get to sleep at three o'clock in the morning, starting at your toes and working your way up to your forehead, tense each muscle, hold it for fifteen seconds, and release it. Even if you don't drift off immediately, you will be more relaxed. If this doesn't work, call a friend in Europe. It will be daytime there.

And this is something else to think about. I understand the importance of long gossipy gatherings with your friends, but rather than spending those hours over Mocha Frappuccinos and Maple Nut scones at Starbucks or lingering over cheese ravioli and tiramisu lunches at the local Italian restaurant, go to the gym and tell your stories while you're working out on the elliptical machine. And when you're spending vacations at the beach, take time out from the "fashion dos and don'ts" pages of *Glamour* magazine and go for a run, or at least an invigorating walk. At least once a day.

Osteoporosis, heart disease, and arthritis are terms that are far from your mind right now, but that won't always be true. And I want to see my girl standing straight and tall and healthy. For the rest of her very long life.

What about dieting? My friends and I spend a lot of time talking about it. You don't diet and you're not overweight.

That's because when I have lunch or dinner anywhere, at home or out, I rarely finish everything on my plate. I have noticed, when I'm having dinner or lunch with friends, that those who constantly talk and worry about their weight do eat every single piece of food that is set in front of them. You can enjoy a large variety of foods, as long as you don't consume them all at one sitting.

And when you go out to dinner, rather than ordering an appetizer and a main course, just ask for two appetizers. They will fill you up and should be satisfying enough. You can have a couple of bites of a chocolate bar to assuage your chocolate cravings; just limit yourself.

A mistake that many women make is discussing the state of their stomach and thighs, not in front of men but with other women. I said to one friend, "If you don't talk about your stomach sticking out, no one will notice it, but if you keep it up, that's exactly what people will focus on." She didn't listen to me but I was right.

What do you think about having plastic surgery?

I think it's fine. I've had a few tweaks and will certainly think about having a more extensive procedure when I run out of turtlenecks. You're a bit young to be thinking about this but it should be considered if someone wants to have her nose fixed or her ears pinned back, her saggy eyelids tightened or the bags under her eyes removed. There are also many nonsurgical crease and wrinkle fillers and muscle relaxers to be considered. Just make certain that you choose a certified plastic surgeon, preferably not someone whose office is in a shopping mall.

I was always afraid that when I did tell you that I was engaged, I would have no idea if you were happy or sad because, thanks to your Botox injections, there's very little expression on your face.

That's not true. I can still curl my upper lip to show my disapproval.

10

language and
grammar

and one more thing . . .

I know exactly what you're going to say, which is why I moved out of your house and into my own apartment. I'd rather live without curtains than listen to you tell me not to use "impact" as a verb.

Well, tough darts, Missy. I can't emphasize strongly enough the importance of the rules governing language and grammar. We stay alive by adapting and changing, but there is an essential structure that we have to observe before everything comes tumbling down around us. Grammatical rules are necessary for simplicity, clarity, and accuracy. They simplify your life and enable you to be as direct and clear as possible in conversation or when you're writing a college admissions essay, a résumé, or a "Dear John" letter. My advice is:

➤ Try never to utter the sentence, "I started babysitting William before I graduated college." Prepositions have feelings, too, you know. You started babysitting *for* William before you graduated *from* college. Schools don't graduate, people do.

➤ However, prepositions have their place. Don't say, "I'm so happy that you like the new blond streaks in my hair that cost more than a summer rental, but it's really not that big of a deal." Where did the "of" come from? It is not required. "Not that big a deal" will suffice.

➤ Although the "t" in *often* is silent, the "h" in *huge* and *human* is not.

➤ Ralph Lauren's name should sound more like Lauren Bacall's than Sophia Loren's.

➤ What are people thinking when they say, "There's thirty-seven cars parked in my driveway"? Don't they realize that "there's" is a contraction for "there is"? "Is" is a singular verb. "Are" is the proper verb for a plural noun.

➤ The word "literally" means "actually," not "nearly" or "virtually." When people say, "I literally spilled my guts," or "My eyes were literally glued to the television set," they mean they felt *as if* their guts had spilled or their eyes were glued. If they had literally engaged in either of those actions, they would not be engaging in conversation; they would be literally dead. Don't use "literally" incorrectly just to emphasize your point.

➤ Do not say, "Oh, so this is your lovely home." It's too cloying; say "house" instead. "Home" is a concept; "house" is a structure. And say "present," not "gift."

➤ No daughter of mine would ever say, "Me and Bobby are fatigued and we're going to lay down," would she? She would know that people lie down, wouldn't she? And she would never begin a sentence with "me," would she?

➤ Recently, a newscaster discussing the Algonquin Round Table mentioned, "Robert Benchley, Dorothy Parker, and the rest of the literary *hoi polloi*," implying that *hoi polloi* is the elite, the nobility. It is, in fact, a Greek word meaning "the many" and describes the masses or the rabble. Apparently, the newscaster thought the words had a high-flying foreign sound and must, in turn, apply to the gentry.

➤ "Parent," "mother," "father," and "task" are *nouns*. Please remember that if you want your mother to keep on parenting you.

➤ "Sans" is the French word for "without." People say it these days with wild abandon, giving it an American pronunciation. A woman will say, "Oh, my dear, my stomach rumbled all during my upper lip wax, because I'd gone the whole day *sans* lunch." Either pronounce it correctly— "sohn"—or, even better, use "without."

➤ I know that children call their mothers "Mom," but especially among grown-ups, when referring to us, I think "my mother" sounds better than "my mom." When I hear a newscaster reporting on the plight of "single moms," I think I'm really listening to someone under the age of fifteen, commenting from the studio audience of a television talk show on an obscure channel. Spaghetti and sympathy have been replaced by pasta and empathy. Are we prepared to let mother go the way of all flesh, as well?

➤ If you are using the word "forte" to mean strength, it is French and pronounced like "fort"; it's not Italian, it does not apply to music being played loudly, and therefore it is not pronounced "fortay."

➤ And speaking of "fort words," the initial meaning of fortuitous is "accidental," not "fortunate." I think you should use it as it was originally intended.

➤ Right now, you think that you would "literally" like me to disappear off the face of the earth, but I'm hoping you mean "almost," not "actually."

11

manners and
thank-you notes

and one more thing . . .

Why do you always tap the back of my elbow—
and I mean _literally_ tap—when I'm introduced to
someone? Don't you think I'm old enough to
remember to shake hands?

Manners, my dear girl, are simply a method of navigating social occasions with the least amount of pressure and anxiety. If you learn the correct behavior at an early age, you don't have to stop and think about what to do. Manners simplify your life and liberate you so that you can flirt with your dinner partner instead of worrying about what to do with your napkin.

As for the elbow tapping, it's just a habit, I guess, left over from your childhood, but I can't bear it when children don't offer their hands when they're being introduced to someone.

A mother of one of your friends complained once about another family. She said, "I hate to have my child to play at their house because the parents are so formal. They make their children shake hands with me and call me Mrs. McDonell instead of Belinda." I assume that she was letting me know that she also considered me too stiff and punctilious about manners, but they are important. If parents don't teach their children, who will? That mother should have demanded a certain standard of behavior from her daughter. When that child grew up, calling the adults in the college admissions offices by their first names and failing to shake hands with prospective employers and mothers- and fathers-in-law, believe me, she was at a disadvantage compared with her more courteous colleagues. Your brother once brought home a girl who did not stand up when she and I were introduced. She would have furthered her cause if she had.

I've given a great deal of thought to my advice on manners and hope you will appreciate the effort that went into the following:

➤ Thank-you notes make people feel good about themselves and about you and, although you should write them because it's the polite thing to do, thank-you letters have also been known to further a career. Just make certain that the words "Thank You" are not preprinted or inscribed anywhere on the paper you're using. The thank you should come only from you.

➤ An old friend developed a thank-you note shortcut when her son was young. She confided to me, "I just got so tired of asking and begging Bartle to write letters to thank people for his Christmas presents that I sat down and did them all myself. I wrote them with my left hand, so they did look as if they had been written by a second-grader."

and one more thing . . .

➤ When you are sending a thank-you note for a baby present it is ridiculous to write it as if it were being sent by the baby or to sign it with the three-week-old infant's name. Why do some parents do this and whom do they think they're fooling?

➤ If you're diligent about your thank-you notes, maybe someone will give a party in your honor. When that happens, remember that it is not good form to drink from your glass when someone is making a toast to you, unless you also find it attractive when the Academy Award nominees sitting in the audience clap for themselves as their names are announced.

➤ When you're introducing yourself or a friend to someone, always use last names. You're not eight years old anymore.

➤ The phrase "We're not at home" is not necessary on your answering machine. We know you're not at home or if you are, you're not answering.

➤ If you ever leave a milk carton on the dining room table, your mother will know. No labels on the table.

Is it all right to e-mail thank-you notes for parties?

Yes, I think it's just fine . . . Some people take a
dim view of this practice, but it makes sense in
this technological age. Why not? After all, it's the
message, not the medium. It's what you say and
how you say it that pleases the recipient. You can
also e-mail thank-you notes for birthday presents,
but for wedding presents, you should probably
send a formal thank-you note. If you've had dinner
at a friend's house the night before, there is nothing wrong with e-mailing a bread-and-butter letter. And it's much more likely that an e-mail will
actually be written and sent than a letter that has
to be folded, put into an envelope, and stamped.

Sympathy notes should be handwritten, because in most cases, although not all, the person
to whom you are writing might be hurt by what is
perceived as a hurried and not genuinely compas-
sionate note.

If you save your e-mail into files and onto a
backup disc, you will have a journal of the events
of your life that your grandchildren will be able to
read, in chronological order. And that's a pretty
gratifying legacy. Okay, so it's not a villa in the
South of France or an annual invitation to the
Academy Awards and the *Vanity Fair* party after-
ward where all the biggest movie stars in the
world gather to check out each other's dresses and
husbands, but it's something to do on a rainy afternoon.

12

holidays and how to
survive them

and one more thing . . .

~~~~~~~~~~~~~~~~~~~~~~~~~~~~~~~~~~~~~~

Sometimes when I look at your Christmas cards and I don't recognize the people in the photograph, I open it up and I still have no idea because they only printed first names. What's that about?

If you have a photograph on your Christmas card and have your names printed on the card, make sure to include your last name as well. Sometimes it is difficult to remember who everyone is. And although this is one of those issues on which no one agrees, I don't feel it's necessary to have your pet's name also engraved on the card.

If you buy your Christmas tree on a Wednesday, don't plan on decorating it until Thursday. You must allow twenty-four hours for the branches to fall to know how the tree will ultimately look and which branches can bear the weight of the ornaments.

Whatever. What do you think of making charitable donations in someone's name and giving that as a Christmas or birthday present?

When a friend specifically asks for that, then it's a fine idea. In general, I think that the person who makes the contribution does it in his or her name, for his or her charity, and the donor gets the credit from the charity and the recipient gets nothing, unless the donation is made to the recipient's charity. And if you think that donating money to a Bolivian fish orphanage in a child's name for a birthday or Christmas present will help that young child to understand the importance of philanthropy, you've lost your mind. Donate if you wish for children, but give them a present as well. Philanthropy separates us from the wild animals, but do it on your own. Get the credit and response that you deserve, but not in place of buying a present for another.

Whew. You're very thorough. When couples get married, they sometimes go crazy driving between her family and his family to celebrate various holidays, especially Christmas and Thanksgiving. It's exhausting but they don't want to disappoint anybody.

When you marry and have children, spend some of the holidays at your own house. Many adult children bring their families to the grandparents and this doesn't seem quite fair to the grandchildren. Your children deserve to have their own yearly traditions that they celebrate in their own living room and dining room. Go to the grandparents on Christmas Eve and let the grandparents come to you for Christmas morning.

Actually, one can make a very strong case for interfaith marriages simply to deal with this dilemma. If a wife is Jewish and her husband is Catholic, they can spend Thanksgiving with her parents and Christmas with his and can avoid the hurt feelings and cranky in-laws altogether. Or at least until it's time for the First Communion or the Bar Mitzvah.

13

conversation and why it's okay to discuss politics

and one more thing . . .

I know, I know, the proudest moment of your life, except when you danced with Duke Ellington, was when you were placed on the Nixon White House enemies list. What else is important?

Voting. Of course, registering so that you are allowed to vote is most important, but it's my opinion that you should register as either a Democrat or a Republican. This business of people signing on as an Independent is pretty lame. You should be *for* something, not on the fence. People who don't vote have no right to whine and carry on about the failures of their government and elected officials.

Independents always sound self-righteous to me when they say, "I vote for the person, not the party." Give me a break. We have a two-party system in this country that I think we should continue. In a democracy, citizens should have an opinion and they should express it. Just because you register as a Democrat does not mean that you can't vote for a Republican candidate in a general election. It is only during the primaries in some states that you have to vote for the candidate of the party in which you registered, but I think you can live with that. You have to affiliate to be effective, in politics as well as in life.

There is, to me, almost nothing more exciting than working in a political campaign. Whether I was working for candidates for the presidency or the city council, I felt that no one could be having a more exhilarating experience than I was. There was no place I would rather have been than with my coworkers, trying to elect a person whom we thought could change the country. I would hope that everyone could have this experience at least once in their lives.

If the voting is the important thing, why did you have to lie down when I told you I was thinking of registering as a Republican?

I never dreamed you would take me so literally. Hypothetically I meant it, but when it came to my own flesh and blood (whom I had carried to full term during the hottest months of the summer), I wanted you to vote the way I do. As a Democrat. I often wonder where I went wrong with you and your political opinions. When you were a baby, I tried to comfort you on colicky nights by walking back and forth in your bedroom, holding you and crooning "Where Have All the Flowers Gone" and "I Am Woman, Hear Me Roar." If I'd known then how you were going to turn out, I'd have just gone with some old favorites from Up with People.

You learned to walk around our dining room table while members of my women's collective addressed envelopes, trying to raise money for a bombed-out hospital in North Vietnam during the

Vietnam War. I pulled you out of pre–nursery
school one day, strapped you into your stroller,
and took you to an "Impeach Nixon" rally. And for
what? So you could date Republicans?

I like Republicans.

Of course you do. They dress well and they're good
dancers, which they should be since they spend
their entire childhood in dancing school. But
there's more to life than the box step and the second floor at Brooks Brothers.

Oh, really? Like what? Those girls in the
alternative lifestyle dorm who went crazy because
my hairspray was in an aerosol can? You know,
you could always tell the Democrats when I was
in school. The girls, anyway. They were the ones
who didn't shave their legs.

Listen, my sweet girl, you're undoubtedly right
about one thing. It is difficult to imagine a Republican who doesn't shave her legs, but there's more
to what I'm trying to explain than that. Maybe
it's the time in which I came of age that has made
me so partisan, but I helped organize the Morato-
rium in New York City and Washington, D. C.,
protest days when people refused to go to work or

school and marched against the war in Vietnam. I gave money to candidates who felt the way I do about the issues. And for this, I was considered a traitor to my country by President Nixon and his cohorts.

I've always wondered about something. What do you wear on a protest march?

You're right. Stick with the Republicans. I think you've found your niche.

Yeah, well, some of my friends never read the paper or watch the news on television. You hate that, don't you?

Oh, I can't stand it. Whether or not you choose to participate in a political movement is your decision, but you must read the newspapers, every day, either online or in the flesh, and know what's going on in the world. And not having time is no excuse. You can listen to the news in your car driving back and forth to work or on your earphones while riding the bus. I think that adults have an obligation to be well informed; there is absolutely no excuse for not being up-to-date on current events.

And speaking very subjectively, you will not do

yourself any favors in your career if it becomes
known that you have no knowledge or interest in
the domestic and international issues that face us
every day.

14

the clueless girl's guide to the sporting life

and one more thing . . .

In the past whenever I had a serious boyfriend, or started dating someone I really liked, I wound up either having to watch sports events with him or to listen to him talk about sports. I would have beer and chips and salsa on hand for him and his friends, but if the occasion arose when he wanted to discuss this stuff with me at half-time or the seventh-inning stretch (whatever that is) I didn't know what to talk about that would make me sound like someone who shared the same interests in whatever game we were watching. How little do I have to know to get by?

Several years ago, when your brother and I were out in the backyard, tossing a football around on a warm summer night and he yelled, "Go long, Mom, go long," I yelled back, "What's wrong with my skirt?" I didn't know that he wanted me to run out for a forward pass; I thought he wanted me to lower the hem on my dress.

If you genuinely want to learn about The Curse of the Bambino and other sports mysteries as well as stats and facts, I've gathered some anecdotes and information that will help explain what the men—and some of the women—in your life are talking about. Certain aspects are truly quite engrossing and if you want to be remembered as more than just another woman who didn't know how to go long, read it. You won't weep.

field guide to games and athletic competitions

Golf. Ask your men friends if they can elaborate on or explain the following sentences. Their responses will provide you with a narrow but interesting backdrop on the game of golf.

"You drive for show, but you putt for dough."

"Ben Crenshaw was a world-class putter, but nobody plays out of bunkers like Ernie Els."

"I love to see John Daly on the tee, the way he grips it and rips it. But of course, nobody gets out of trouble like Tiger."

Baseball. It's a long season of about 160 games, plus the play-offs and world series; it really is a three-season game, excluding winter, so you might inquire into the following topics. Men are usually either Boston Red Sox or New York Yankee fans, even if they're from Los Angeles and love the Dodgers or Milwaukee and root for the Braves, so if he loves the Yankees, ask about the Curse of the Bambino and whether the Bosox can ever win *another* Series. If he's a Red Sox guy, learn about "breaking up the Yankees" and the days when the Boston Braves had only two pitchers they could rely on and when the poetry of Fenway Park was, "Spahn and Sain and pray for rain." When the Braves owner took his team and decamped to Milwaukee, they said of him in Beantown (Boston), "This is dear old Boston, the home of the cod and the beanie, where the Lowells speak only to Cabots and nobody speaks to Perini." (If he likes the Red Sox, he'll probably propose to you after this.)

Thanks, Mommy. I'm starting to pray for rain.

Oh, I'm not done yet. Stats are a whole new world, but you could begin by learning about how Mark McGwire broke Roger Maris's home run record and Roger broke Babe Ruth's record of sixty home runs in one season. Of course, Barry Bonds soon broke McGwire's record, and Henry Aaron, a.k.a. Hammerin' Hank, broke The Babe's *total* H.R. record of 714. But you knew that.

Basketball. College hoops are dominated by Duke and Stanford. If you score a three-point goal, which is a shot from far-out, you have scored from "downtown." If you make a lay-up in a close shot, you have scored "in the paint."

Football. It's all about trying to get the ball to cover some part of one hundred yards, and ruin some very lush green grass, to score a touchdown that is worth six points. After a touchdown, the team can score one point by kicking the ball through the goalposts or two points by running or passing it into the end zone. "The Game" is Harvard versus Yale. The important rivalry in the Big Ten is between Ohio State and Michigan.

Once you know the basic facts about sports, you can watch the games with him, discuss the final scores, and you may actually find yourself engrossed in the process. I love the Boston Red Sox and I still don't really understand why they didn't win a World Series between 1918 and 2004. Maybe it wasn't Babe Ruth, the Bambino of the Curse. Maybe we should look in other directions.

15

women friends and
men friends and
keeping them happy

and one more thing . . .

My friends are so important to me but I worry sometimes that when I get married, my relationship with them might change.

It's a legitimate worry but you don't have to let it happen. A girlfriend helps you through the best of times and the worst of times. You can tell her about your promotion at work. She can tell you about the setup with a guy who not only showed up at the restaurant two and a half hours late, but who—when he did appear—was drunk and with another girl. True friends will be thrilled to hear about your successful career and will provide a sympathetic ear when you describe your nights from hell.

And as we all know, it's your women friends who provide meaningful and accurate information on other people. If you need to learn the real dope on someone, a woman can do background checks to rival the CIA. A man, on the other hand, could have dinner with another couple and fail to mention that the wife never spoke to her husband during the evening, had dyed her previously auburn hair black, and appeared to be about six months' pregnant. Men are cute but they can be a bit lax on details.

When you become a mother and your three-year-old child bites her nursery school teacher on the leg, your sixteen-year-old daughter gets drunk and passes out at the high school dance, and your twenty-year-old flunks out of college for the third time, there will be some people with whom you will not be inclined to share this information. Then there are those whom you will rush to tell, and who will comfort you and assure you that, like a haircut gone wrong, this too will pass. Treasure the last group. They're your true friends.

(Of course, there is usually one woman around who can pass the Ladies' Room Test. I refer to those girls about whom you can speak honestly and sometimes quite unsympathetically in a public ladies room, confident in the knowledge that no matter how many unknown women are in the stalls, not one of them will ever storm out in high dudgeon, furious at you for criticizing her good friend and willing to defend her name at any cost. Those girls you have spoken about have no best friends so you're always safe.)

So in general, women are more reliable than men?

Yes, in many areas, but once in a while, even they can let you down. Many years ago, between marriages, I invited three friends to dinner. One week before our get-together, a devastatingly attractive man asked me to a Beach Boys concert. I turned him down, of course, because what kind of woman would abandon her woman friends for a man? My guests, apparently, because by the night of the dinner, all three had ditched me for men.

My married friend's husband wanted her to stay home with him because he was bored and couldn't fix his own dinner. The other two were asked out on dates. I think my married friend should have told her husband to watch the basketball play-offs and fix himself some dinner, and if he still had some spare time, he could clean out the refrigerator. As for the other two women, I've learned that there are no absolutes in life. While it is clearly bad form to break dates if something better comes along, there are exceptions. If the opportunity for dinner at the White House presents itself, or tickets to a play that will be closing the next day, or an evening with Jude Law, then I think you should explain it to your hostess, who should, in turn, let you off the hospitality hook.

As for that night years ago, maybe if I had canceled my dinner and gone to the concert, none of *my* guests would have been upset. And my eyes would not still fill with tears when I hear "Surfer Girl" and think of what might have been.

I start to cry when I hear any Beach Boys song, too, because I know you're going to tell that story again. You have a lot of gay men friends. Do they ever ditch you?

Never. I count on those men friends as much as I do my women friends. And they've stood by me when their straight male counterparts didn't. They gave me advice and consolation and many laughs during times of divorce, remarriage, career changes, new babies, and new curtains in the living room. And, when my under-eye concealer or my hair colorist failed to do their jobs, my gay friends told me in the kindest way. (Well, most of them, anyway.) Your brother once said, "You're the only mother I know who really wouldn't mind if she had a gay son."

Okay, why am I not surprised to hear that? Maybe because you were also the only mother who would call my college dorm and say, "Why do you girls limit yourselves to only dating white boys?" You look so normal, and I never know what you're going to say next. But there is a lot of diversity among your friends. I mean, not just older women, but gay men. I think it's cool. I hope I have an equally diverse group of close friends when I'm your age.

I hope you do, too. Your life will be richer for it. Or maybe it won't. A gay English friend once asked me how I was preparing to deal with my empty nest once my children were both off at college. I told him that my future plans included a facelift and a trip to Graceland. There was a pause, after which I figured he would assure me that I shouldn't even consider having plastic surgery on my taut and youthful face, and that he hoped I would enjoy visiting Elvis's Jungle Room. But he said, "Oh, forget Graceland, Luv, have the bloody facelift."

What should I do if I see my best friend's husband in an out-of-the-way restaurant with another woman, and it's clear that it's not a business lunch? Shouldn't I tell her?

No. The discovery process is accidental but the damage that can be done by informing your friend is significant. It's a matter to be dealt with, or not, by the people involved, not you. Sometimes the wife is fully aware of the man's wandering ways and has made a decision—because she doesn't consider it serious or because she doesn't want to be alone or to bring up her children without a father—to ignore it. So why would you make her life miserable and difficult?

Because if I didn't tell her, and she found out that I had known about it, she would never forgive me.

My advice is it's better to take a chance and not cause her the initial pain. Just make sure you're around to support her if she does eventually learn of it. For all you know, you could be witnessing the end of an affair that never would have become known to your friend. Playing God is not an act of friendship.

What do you do if you outgrow a friend or just have nothing in common with her any more? Can you break up with her?

Unless someone has committed an act of unspeakable thoughtlessness, I think it's too painful for all concerned if you get on your high horse and cut her off completely. It takes considerable effort and emotion to refuse to speak to someone. It's easier and more humane to be pleasant when you see her, ease up on phone calls, e-mails, and intimate lunches and limit your invitations to her to big cocktail parties.

Unforeseen events change people's lives and you might want to be close once again, so leave the door open and don't hurt an old friend's feelings. Unless she's stolen your husband, your boyfriend, or your new diamond stud earrings.

My high school reunion is in three months. Do you think I should go?

Oh, yes, go. From my experience in the world of high school and college reunions, you'll regret it if you don't go. It's exhilarating to see everyone again and always gratifying to hear that the girl from the ninth grade who told you to wear your patchwork prairie skirt to the movies with her— and never told you that she had also invited some cool boys and she was wearing tight jeans and a cool top—has been indicted for insider trading at her first job. You have nothing to lose by attending, especially at your young age when you won't have to lie awake nights, wondering if you can have your jawline microsuctioned and still be able to afford transportation to the reunion. Take advantage of your youth.

16

men and how to survive them

Do you think it's true that when a group of women go out together for the evening, they spend the entire time discussing men but they don't want to be with them, and when men go out at night, they never talk about women but they're always looking for some to join them?

Absolutely, and I don't know why. And I'll tell you something else that is incomprehensible to me. There is no such thing as a man another woman doesn't want. Every man in prison has a girlfriend or is married. Or both. Even the men on death row have pen pals to whom they eventually become engaged and marry over the telephone.

Putting felons aside, I could never seriously consider spending my life with any man who didn't know more than I do about history, baseball, and blazers, and less than I do about the British royals and the lyrics to every rock 'n' roll song written during the sixties.

Are there some qualities that are common to men?

Oh, my dear, where to begin? I've thoughtfully prepared a partial and very subjective list:

➤ If you're shopping for clothes with a man and you decide to try something on, your first inclination might be to ask your companion to watch your handbag while you're in the dressing room. Don't do it. It's not that he will refuse. On the contrary, he will accept his responsibility with grace. "Just leave it right here," he'll say with comforting assurance. The minute you leave to go to your dressing room, something or someone will catch his eye. He will stroll away, leaving your bag accessible to any thief who wanders along. He doesn't do this deliberately; it's simply that men do not have the pocketbook gene. They, unlike women, don't understand how to keep an inanimate object in their sights.

➤ Men never understand, even after years of marriage, why women don't want to be kissed while they're in the kitchen dicing onions for the pot roast, in the bathroom putting on their mascara, or leaving the house after putting on fresh lipstick.

➤ I strongly urge you to keep your distance from any man who looks beamingly at his wife and says, "We're pregnant." And don't even ask me to discuss the husband who recounts those long, agonizing hours "when *we* were in labor."

➤ To avoid four and a half minutes standing still in traffic, a man will drive seventy-three miles out of his way, simply to keep moving. This same man will not complain when given a windowless hotel room with two army cots and a sink in the closet.

Could a man make up a similar list about women?

It would never occur to a man to make a list like this. They don't think the way we do. And they don't always like to go to the same places we like. Two years ago, I dragged your stepfather to Las Vegas. On the last night of our short stay, I took him to see Wayne Newton in concert at a hotel on the Strip. I was in heaven, listening to Wayne belt out one great song after another. It wasn't until he was singing "Lay a Little Lovin' on Me," that I noticed my escort had dozed off. When the band geared up with a particularly loud blast of music, he awoke with a start. Looking at him sympathetically, I said, "You hate Wayne Newton, don't you?"

"No," he answered evenly, "I hate you for bringing me here," and went right back to sleep.

the clotheshorse man or harassed tweed

What about men who are as interested in their clothes as I am in mine?

You may find yourself besotted with a man who considers blazers and tasseled loafers to be among the world's great inventions and spends hours ruminating over whether his shirts should be hung up or folded. He also refuses to fly on the same plane with his tailor because if it crashed, who would look after his lapels? Fall in love with him, if you must, but with the caveat that if you marry him, he'll have more closets than you do. And they'll be deeper.

But try to be grateful as you realize that this man will never show up anywhere in a tank top. For that, you should help him fold his silk pocket squares. Of course, if you notice that he's packing a bathrobe for a camping trip, his tasseled loafers could begin to get on your nerves.

You must also be aware that on some summer night, when you and he are wandering around the slippery docks of a boat marina in the pitch dark, he will not utter the words, "I love you and here's a new bracelet I just bought you." What he will say is, "Don't fall in the water because I'm not jumping in after you and wrecking my new blazer."

Are there really significant differences among the men whom you've known, in terms of different religions and backgrounds? And do the differences really matter?

Well, they don't matter in any global sense. But there are a few minor differences among men in terms of religion and background that are worthy of discussion. The men I've loved, gone out with, ditched, been dumped by, married, had children with, and divorced have been from the Northeast, and had fairly nonobservant Christian or Jewish backgrounds. So I will concentrate on the divisions between these groups. If I'd had any experience with Muslims from Missouri or born-again Baptists from Boise, I'd tell you about it. But I can only talk about what I know. Most of the time.

the wasp man

Let's start with white Anglo-Saxons. Are they all the same?

No, they can be either quite high-flown, middle-class, or working at the Dairy Queen in Toad Suck, Arkansas. Of these, the high-flown man is the most intriguing.

His mother told him that when he received a printed invitation, he could determine whether or not the lettering was engraved or—*quelle horreur*—"merely raised," by running his fingers along the back. If the invitation was embossed and not engraved, he should send his heartfelt regrets. "Merely raised" to a WASP mother is akin to setting the table and placing the fork directly on the napkin.

When you have dinner in a restaurant with the High-WASP Man and his friends, you won't be able to put your feet flat on the floor because of all the coats that are piled up. Why pay a dollar to have your coat checked when you can just toss it under the table?

You'll have to force him to see a doctor. Seeking medical advice, with its prospect of actually discussing his body with someone and maybe even having blood taken, comes about as easily to him as throwing out his ten-year-old, lime-green linen pants with the mallard duck appliqués up the sides. And, if that weren't bad enough, he has to pay for it.

If you receive a phone call from him before five o'clock in the afternoon, expect the worst. He will never call before the rates change, unless someone is in a coma. Or unless he has a cell phone, in which case he will call on weekends and after nine. Except that he considers cell phones to be nothing more than a toxic public nuisance so don't count on him to own one.

Don't expect more than stunned silence when you point out to him that jewelry is not like kitchen equipment. Unlike double boilers, where one suffices, having one piece of jewelry doesn't mean you won't need another.

the jewish man, or "you can always tell the shiksas at a seder. they only eat the hard-boiled eggs"

Now that you have a Jewish husband, what have you learned? How is he different from the WASP?

For one thing, his questions are different. You'll never hear a Roman Catholic or a Methodist inquire of a woman or a wife, "Are you going to be warm enough in that?" Or to ask, several times a week, "Are you sure you have enough food?" Or, in the middle of an overcast summer afternoon when the sun's rays haven't been glimpsed since the previous day, to insist, "Even though it's cloudy today, you can still get a hell of a burn. Are you using your sunblock?"

Jewish men do ask these questions, due to their real fear that a loved one might somehow be caught in a freak snowstorm in late spring and, right on the sidewalk in front of a supermarket, be forced to drink melted snow before simultaneously freezing and starving to death. With a severe sunburn.

If you marry him, you'll learn to live with dire health conditions. He will never be cold, he will have frostbite; he will not get thirsty, he will be dehydrated; he will not cough, he will choke.

If you have children together, he will be the only father at Blarney Castle in Ireland, admonishing his offspring not to kiss the Blarney stone, saying, "You could get a cold sore from that filthy thing."

You'll learn not to be alarmed when he begins a sentence with "You know what my mother always said, don't you?" The answer is usually along the lines of, "Only common people like salted butter."

But what can be expected from a man whose mother's explanation to her eight-year-old son when they spotted two dogs mating, was the following: "The little dog on the bottom is sick and the big dog on top is pushing her to Mount Sinai Hospital."

I once overheard a couple on the sidewalk behind me engaged in the following conversation.

The man said, "You know, my mother would be mad at me today."

The woman asked, "Why?"

He said, "Because I've dressed for the weather, not the season."

She said, "Well, your mother was wrong. That

doesn't make any sense. It's ridiculous to dress for the season and not the weather."

He paused and then said, "She wasn't wrong about one thing. She told me never to marry a shiksa."

all other men

Since you asked, darling, even though I'm not expert on the subject of All Other Men, my life experience is broad enough that I can hazard a few generalities.

How is it I could see this coming?

If you meet a man at a party and he says, "That's my wife over there. She's more beautiful today than on the day we got married. My God, I'm so in love with her," he's having an affair.

The same man who says that he can't marry you because you want children and he doesn't will eventually marry another woman and will have children with her. It never fails.

Nothing favorable has ever resulted from a man saying, "I've got something to discuss with you and now is just as good a time as any." Whenever I hear that sentence, I go straight to the kitchen and alphabetize the spice rack.

dating but not by those rules

and one more thing . . .

Mommy, what would you tell an unmarried woman about dating and love? Do you think that sooner or later a guy will break her heart?

Yes, it's just a part of life. You can't do much about it. There are a few strategies that might be helpful in some cases. When a man whom you do like—in spite of the fact that he seems oblivious to your existence for weeks on end—finally calls you, keep two ideas firmly in mind as you talk to him: *cheerful* and *busy*. Tell him you're busy and will call him right back and then don't. After you do this a couple of times, he'll go crazy trying to get in touch with you. This usually works in any situation where the man is not being as attentive as you would wish him to be. I hate having to say this, but it's true. Pretend you have a life, even if you don't. Being elusive is the only tactic that works with some men. Okay, most men. If, when he does call you, you sound sad and needy because you haven't heard from him, he will undoubtedly be sweet and sympathetic but he will not think of you when he wants to have a lighthearted and relaxed night on the town. Remember, pathetic isn't sexy.

That's it? There are no other options?

She could knock herself out in an effort to make his life with her so wondrously enjoyable that he won't ever want to be anywhere else, but frankly, I'd go with elusive. It's much less exhausting.

Many women view all men as potential husbands. Men do not think of women that way until they have made the decision to marry. *Then* they look at the women they're dating at that moment as potential wives.

So it's all in the timing?

I think so. I am also wary of romantic relationships that proceed too smoothly. In my experience, some strife, some unsettling periods, some times when you think you may not end up with the man of your dreams (and you don't know how you'll face the rest of your life without him, but you ultimately win him) are essential to a full-blown love affair. When a tempestuous liaison eventually works, it can be very satisfying.

I feel it incumbent upon me to raise a delicate and questionable subject for a mother, but one that I do feel deserves a hearing. In this complicated world of human relationships, it is possible for a woman to fall in love with a man who is married. And it's also conceivable that he might be married to someone who truly doesn't understand him or like him or love him. In which case, if she and he do love each other, it would be a pity to give it up just because, in general, "one does not date married men."

It's my experience that women who are unhappy in their marriages often simply leave their husbands and live by themselves, perfectly content, and yes, often ecstatic, to be alone. Men, who don't often share this delight, tend to stay on long after they should have gone. No man, to my knowledge, has ever considered uttering the following words: "Gosh, my marriage is a disaster. I think I'd better end it now, move out, and spend some time on my own, thinking about what went wrong. I'll move to a small apartment, attend to household details like buying SOS pads to put under the sink and making sure I have some place to store the bacon fat, and after that, I'll spend the day in quiet reflection." Men are far more familiar with ESPN than they are with quiet reflection. They also, as a rule, don't leave one woman until there's another waiting in the car with an empty Chock full o'Nuts coffee can for the bacon fat.

The effect of this less than admirable behavior is that the majority of men are attached to a woman at most points in their lives. To think of a man as out of the running, simply because he's married, is short-sighted. Men are always married. Once they get started, they can't stop. (I am not, of course, advocating running off with your friends' husbands as some kind of thoughtless game, and please remember, whatever you do, lives will be thrown into chaos.)

Now what are you telling me? That married men are fair game?

No, I'm not telling you that at all. What I am saying is that one can't plan for life's random events. But having some rules can help. Although sometimes they don't. My husband once sat beside a woman at a dinner party who told him that she'd had three husbands. She added, "Some people said I married every man I ever kissed." He said, "That's interesting. I think my wife kissed every married man she ever met."

Okay, enough about married men. What about going dutch when you go out on a date?

I think that each person paying his or her share of the restaurant bill is fine, especially if you're platonic friends. Or sometimes the person who asks the other to go out wants to treat. As you grow older, some men will choose to take responsibility for most of the restaurant dates. Unless, of course, they're starving poets or are putting their orphaned younger siblings through college, and the girl is an heiress and she demands to pay. I think, in the great scheme of life, which sometimes includes eating in restaurants, going dutch still makes the most sense. People can take turns treating each other for birthdays and celebrations, but if their method of payment is kept on an equal basis, it's easier for everyone. And each person has a say in choosing a restaurant and this sometimes gives you the freedom to go to one that's new, hot, and expensive.

If a guy calls on Wednesday to ask a girl out for Friday night, should she accept? Does she seem like a loser to go out on such short notice?

Of course she should go out with him and she absolutely won't seem like a loser. She'd be a loser if she missed out on an evening that could be fun and interesting.

But you said a girl should act as if she's very busy.

Yes, but that's only if the man whom she likes seems to be losing interest and she wants to draw him back. But if there is no undercurrent of discontent and no reason to get crafty with him, there is also no reason not to go out with him. He'll just keep calling girls until he finds someone who'll go out with him. If he calls a girl on Saturday afternoon to go out with him that night, she should go if she wants to. It's her decision. If she likes him, refusing to see him because of the timing of his call makes no sense at all. But if she accepts a date with him and they go to a cocktail party, she should avoid the smoked salmon canapé. Unless she is carrying a toothbrush, toothpaste, and a box of Altoids in her bag.

How do you break up with a guy?

Once you've decided that you no longer want to be with the guy you've been dating, the noble thing to do is to break it off as soon as possible. You clearly want the opportunity to meet someone you'd be happier with, and he deserves the same. You should be as truthful and kind as possible when explaining why you should no longer be together. I think you could say that no one knows what the future holds, that maybe you'll get together again, but for now, you think you should see other people. And don't use him to go out with until you meet someone else, just because you can't be alone. That's not fair to him and unworthy of you.

You'll always have a better relationship with the men you ditch than with those who ditch you. Years later, when you run into one of them at your college reunion, there will always be a trace of yearning for what they could never have. The men who leave you will also be pleasant when you see them, but it will be out of either guilt or relief.

What if someone falls in love with a guy and he really can't commit? How long should she wait around for him?

I think a time limit should be set. If a girl is madly in love with a guy and he knows that she would like to marry but feels he isn't ready yet, and they've been together for at least a year, she should say to herself: "I'm going to give him six months. I won't drive him crazy and talk about it all the time, but if he seems obviously uninterested or afraid after that period of time, then I will hit the road and find someone else who wants what I want." Don't tell him that you've set up this mental ultimatum. It's a deadline just for you to be aware of and will help you through the months ahead and keep the arguing and frustration to a minimum. If he doesn't come around, there's no reason for you to stick around. There are many men in this world with whom a woman can fall in love, not just one.

Or as a college friend from Texas used to say, "Just because we're chained to the porch doesn't mean we still can't bark at the postman."

Peculiarly stated but yes.

I have several friends from college who aren't even dating anybody, let alone finding someone to marry, and they're getting kind of nervous and depressed about it. What would you say to them?

First, I would suggest that they read the wedding announcement section of the Sunday *New York Times*. Ages of the newlywed couples are given and the majority of the brides are from very late twenties to middle thirties, with even some in their seventies. I would also remind them that they should savor this moment. For the only time in their lives, they're liberated and free of husbands, children, needy or ailing parents. This is when they can figure out what they want to do with themselves and have fun doing it. I would advise them not to sit around in their apartments after work, talking about how they're going to end up unmarried, like Alice on *The Brady Bunch,* and to get out there. Volunteer to work on a political campaign or tutor children in an after-school program. Take swing dancing lessons or learn to make pottery. There's a whole world full of variety and this is your time to take advantage of it.

18

sex

(the shortest chapter)

and one more thing . . .

~~~~~~~~~~~~~~~~~~~~~~~~~~~~~~~~~~~~~

I can't believe what you said about married men, so I don't even want to know what you have to say about sex.

> Relax, darling. My first rule would be not to fill your mother in on all the grisly details.

Do you think a couple should move in together when they become engaged or wait until they are married?

> It's my opinion that they should move in with each other. You never really know someone until you've actually lived with him. Or her. I don't see the point in waiting since they want to be together and will be. Also, practically speaking, why should people pay the rent on two apartments when they spend all their time together anyway?

How soon should you wait to have sex with someone you're dating?

> I think it depends. Sometimes you can go to bed with a man on the second or third date and end up happily married for the next fifty years. You could also date someone for six months and know in your heart that sleeping with him would be a mistake and something that you would regret doing.
> If it feels right and you want to do it, and you're

protecting yourself from pregnancy and sexually transmitted diseases, why not? No one would ever ask a man this same question. I think this is a flexible situation that you have to judge for yourself.

Which reminds me: when you're a middle-aged woman and run into a man whom you used to know and you can't remember whether or not you slept with him, you did.

Why is this the shortest chapter?

Because I'm your mother.

19

weddings

and one more thing . . .

You're always so critical about people's weddings. I hope you'll lighten up for mine.

I know that you will want to make your own personal imprint on your wedding but don't go too far afield. I'll lighten up on your wedding day if you go along with me on the following points:

➤ Refer to the men who attend the groom as ushers. After noting, with some dismay, the advent of the word *groomsmen* or even worse, *groomspersons,* and the gradual disappearance of the word *ushers,* I've decided that the term "groomsmen" should be used only for those men who are leading horses to the wedding ceremony.

➤ Do not suggest black dresses for your bridesmaids, ever. For any reason. Black is for funerals and cocktail parties, not wedding parties. I once had the great misfortune of attending a wedding with a black-and-white color scheme. I thought the bridesmaids' dresses, black satin and tulle, were in debatable taste, until I went into the ladies' room and saw, in a basket on the sink counter, individual Tampax tubes, each lovingly and thoughtfully tied with black satin ribbon. When the bride's sister married the following year, I claimed PMS and stayed home.

➤ Although this is a minor complaint, do not use a Love or Cupid stamp on the reply envelope of the wedding invitation; it is too cloying. A wildflower or Cary Grant stamp would be a better choice.

➤ Realize that some people feel very strongly that the bride should not send out reply cards with the invitations. They think that the guests should write a proper response to the parents who are giving the wedding, stating whether or not they will be attending. I was a part of this movement until I heard from several mothers of brides and from brides themselves who reported that many people don't reply at all unless they can fill in their names on the blank line of the enclosed card and check off whether or not they will grace the occasion. You can either be a stickler for the proper etiquette, which would be my first response, or you could enclose printed reply cards with the invitations. By doing this, you will receive prompt responses, which will mean far fewer sleepless nights as you work on the menu and the seating arrangement. Do not include a meat or fish choice to be checked off on the reply card. It's just too unappealing for words. There should be some surprises left at a wedding.

➤ Be clear about this: Even if the bride's family is paying for the wedding, her parents should not limit the number of guests whom the groom's parents may invite. It's humiliating and unfair to the groom's family. This is a party to celebrate the members of two families. You can't have vast numbers of people from one side and not the other.

➤ Be aware that after the invitations have been mailed, you may discover someone you didn't invite has hurt feelings because he or she expected to be asked. If it's only a few individuals and it's not a great financial or seating hardship, invite them. It's less trouble for you and they will be so appreciative. If you don't ask them, you will live with their sad or angry positions for years to come. It's not worth it. If your wedding is large enough, you won't even know that they're there. But they will.

➤ Think long and hard before writing your own wedding vows. If you have personal thoughts and intimate words for each other, perhaps you could share them over drinks after your engagement party or during your honeymoon, but are they really for the world to hear? *The Book of Common Prayer* has survived for a few thousand years for good reason. The words that a presiding judge might read are equally effective. They're both short and sweet, and you won't cringe when you're older while watching the videotape of your own wedding ceremony.

➤ Wait a day between your wedding and leaving on your honeymoon. It's too hectic to go from dancing at your reception to a sleepless night and then the airport. A day in between will allow you a much-deserved and -needed break.

➤ Don't take an extensive honeymoon. I've run into newly married couples who are on their fifth week of traveling alone and they're pining for new people to talk with. Two weeks, then on with your life. You'll also be anxious to get home and gossip about your wedding with your friends. If you go trekking in the Himalayas for five weeks, your wedding day will be very old news by the time you get back.

20

marriage and mothers-in-law

marriage

You have been married a couple of times, so tell me this. Why do magazine articles and marriage counselors on television always say that you have to work on a marriage? What does that mean?

I have no idea why people say that. If you and your husband don't have fun together and don't enjoy each other, all things being equal, what is the rationale for being married?

I don't advocate hitting the road when your husband is sick, broke, or out of a job either. But you shouldn't have to work at your marriage the way you work at your job.

Aren't you supposed to be married to a man because you love him madly and enjoy yourself more being with him than without him? Because he enhances your life? Because you look forward to talking with him, telling him about your day, and finding out what he thinks about world events— and because you love to kiss him? If being married becomes a chore like cleaning the lint trap in the dryer, who needs it?

I have never understood the practice of seeing a marriage counselor with your fiancé before the marriage. If the situation is that precarious and unsettled and you aren't even married, perhaps it was never a sound idea from the beginning.

People talk about the importance of communication in marriage. What does that mean, exactly? It always sounds like such a big deal.

When a marriage works, there's nothing better, but when it doesn't, it's a sad and awful life. People say that communication is of the utmost importance in a marriage and of course, that's true. But if a husband and wife are happy, they look forward to talking with each other at the end of a day, telling sad or funny stories, or just getting each other's opinions. Communication is not something that one has to work on as a project. If a man and a woman love each other, then chatting, gossiping, exchanging ideas and asking for opinions, and laughing and crying together just happens and is part of the deal. And a very worthwhile part, at that.

mothers-in-law

Do you think there's a difference between having a son-in-law and a daughter-in-law?

Absolutely. I think that in a majority of marriages, the wives call the shots in the domestic world, and often they involve their own mothers in their lives to the exclusion of their husbands' mothers. And to the detriment of their children. Children need all four (or in our family of multiple marriages, seven) of their grandparents. Some men, after marriage, are in total thrall to their wives and in the interest of keeping the peace at home, they allow their mothers to become forgotten in the fray.

I talk to so many women whose conversations about their sons' wives and children are always tinged with reticence and caution. These women admit that they are freer expressing their ideas and feelings about their grandchildren to their daughters than to their daughters-in-law. Their great fear is annoying their sons' wives and not being able to play as big a role in their grandchildren's lives as they would hope. It shouldn't be this way. Don't let it happen to you.

Do you think you're just saying this because you're also the mother of a son?

Without a doubt.

21

separation and divorce
and why it's not the
end of the world

Couldn't this wait until I've at least been married for a month?

I hope with all my heart that you and the readers of this book and their future husbands will be gloriously, staggeringly happy. But if your marriages should go awry, here are a few points to ponder.

➤ If, when he travels, your husband says that the hotel phones don't work and he can only be reached by his cell phone or e-mail, he could be having an affair.

➤ If he has all the moles on his back removed, he could be having an affair.

➤ If he covers the annual income section of your joint income tax form with his hand as he asks you to sign it, *you* should be having an affair.

➤ If you are miserably unhappy in your marriage and considering a separation, it's wise to plan ahead in terms of the photographs on your Christmas cards. Sometimes women say, "I'm going to leave my husband but I don't want to do it until after the holidays. It would be too awful for everyone if we were to separate now." That's often due to the fact that after she's had to bribe her children to even sit for the Christmas photos, which she's then spent hours gluing to the actual cards, she's not going to let the whole effort go to waste. When your father and I were nearing the end of our marriage, I had two series of photos taken for our Christmas cards, one of the three of us and one of just you and me. He didn't move out until New Years' Day, so I went with the first batch.

➤ If you do decide to leave your husband, have your windows washed and your hair highlighted before you tell him. For some reason, men are loath to pay for these particular items once they realize that they'll soon be on their own, having to learn the ins and outs of fabric softener.

Shouldn't couples try to stay together if they have children?

I don't know why anyone should stay with another person if they're miserably unhappy. It might be difficult initially for children when their parents separate, but they'll adjust and survive. Staying with a husband or wife in a miserable marriage is just about the dumbest thing I can think of for all concerned.

There is one very promising aspect of divorce that most women don't consider until they've actually gone through the process. When your children spend weekends with their father as part of

the custody agreement, you have a two- or three-
day period when you can take a trip, go to the
movies, or just sit around your house reading
trashy novels. Your children are with their father,
which is the next best thing to being with you.
And you are free of guilt.

I recently found the diary I kept when I was
sixteen years old, when my parents decided to divorce. The entry for March 10 says, *"While
Mommy and I were shopping today, she told me
that she and Daddy are going to get divorced.
That's so sad. We picked out my dress for the Ju-
nior Prom. It's white organza, strapless and has a
big bow in the back, right over the zipper."* And
then I drew a sketch of the dress that seemed to
be so much more important to me than the state
of my parents' marriage. We all survived, I was
not crowned Prom Queen, and even then I realized that the breakup was preferable to the ten-
sion and pressure that we had all been living
with.

Shouldn't everyone involved in an unhappy
family be allowed to have a chance at a better life?
Shouldn't children know what it's like not to live
in a combative or a miserably silent atmosphere?
Their lives won't be the same after a divorce, but
children are more resilient than their parents
credit them with and they will survive. And in
many cases children's lives will improve as much

as their parents'. Children are better off with happy-but-divorced parents than with married-but-miserable ones.

I also don't believe that the knowledge that the parents stayed together only for the children's sake is a legacy that will bring any joy to the children involved. It might make them feel guilty to know that if it weren't for them, their mother and father might have had a chance at a happier life.

Life is too short to continue reading a book you don't enjoy. Take it back to the library or give it away. I feel the same about husbands.

22

pregnancy and babies

and one more thing . . .

I can't believe that anyone like you—who looks as though she could be driving a minivan in Scarsdale—would do something as alternative as having a baby before you were married. And you were the sixth-grade class mother for me that year. Did you have a difficult time with the other parents when you had a son before you were married?

It was tricky at times. Simply explaining to my father that being an unwed, pregnant thirty-five-year-old didn't carry quite the stigma of being an unwed, pregnant high school cheerleader was exhausting. That was the scenario that had kept him awake nights for most of my teenage years. It was nearly as difficult as informing the headmistress of your school that I had taken my job as the sixth-grade class mother rather more seriously than she had expected. But life would have been far trickier if I had never had my boy.

As for my mother, she doesn't care how she gets her grandchildren, as long as she gets them. She held him in her arms during the wedding ceremony. If she'd also been able to nurse him, I could have danced more at the reception.

I firmly expected to be married first and then to get pregnant, but when the divorce negotiations between my second husband and his first wife began to drag on, we decided that our commitment to each other and a desire to have a child superseded any silliness about dates. At one point I told him that if we could marry before our baby started on solid foods, I could handle whatever came to pass. I just never imagined that I'd conceive in less time than it takes me to change the bag in the vacuum cleaner.

A situation like this does provide experience in coping with questions that can become tricky. At a party several months after my son was born, one of the women guests, after hearing that I'd recently given birth, asked "Is this your first baby?"

I nodded cheerfully. "My first illegitimate one, yes."

After delving further, she suggested that I change the date of my wedding anniversary so that my child would not be doomed to suffer because of my loose living. But another woman in the group, the mother of another sixth-grader, patted my shoulder and said, "You've shown our girls that they have options." That made me feel even better than my epidural.

When it happened, I was kind of embarrassed and I still don't think I would have taken the same path, but I do think it's cool that you have more in common with Goldie Hawn and Susan Sarandon than my friends' mothers. Since I was

rather young at the time, refresh my memory.
How did you explain this whole deal to your out-
of-wedlock child?

What I struggled to do was to turn an unwieldy
situation, with the potential for misunderstand-
ing and hurt feelings at some later date, into
something that was just another quirky but en-
dearing aspect of our family. I thought honesty
and humor were the obvious tactics, but I am
afraid that what worked for me was choosing to
tell him about his rakish beginnings when he was
too young to really understand it.

When he was about five, we were looking
through my wedding album and when he ob-
served, "I'm so lucky I was at your wedding. Some
of my friends didn't get to go to their mommies'
weddings," I seized the moment. I carefully ex-
plained that most parents were already married
when their children were born, but his father and
I hadn't been able to marry as soon as we wanted
to. Pressing on, I told him that we'd wanted a
baby so much that we'd gone ahead and had him
anyway and were very happy that we had. I
thought I had struck just the right note and was
feeling pretty smug until his next question, which
was if I had ever wondered why all the triceratops
were dead.

I still have a bunch of friends who have no interest in getting married for quite a few years. They want to concentrate on their careers, but they do want to marry eventually and have children. What do you think of women having babies when they're in their late thirties or early forties?

I have three close friends who gave birth to their first babies when they were in their early to middle forties. The children have thrived and the women have had the time of their lives being their mothers. I don't think age matters when one decides to have a child. With each succeeding generation in this country, mothers have had their first child at an increasingly advanced age. You can be an effective and loving mother at twenty-five or forty-five. I don't understand what age has to do with bringing up children except that older mothers may sometimes be superior parents simply because they've lived longer and experienced more than some of their twenty-five-year-old counterparts. And younger mothers may have more energy for the playground and the water parks.

There are, however, two hitches for those more mellow mamas. When my friend Suzanne became pregnant with her first baby in her mid-forties, her husband, the father of a teenaged son by an earlier marriage, wasn't deeply captivated by the idea of birthing classes, so I volunteered to be her Lamaze coach. The other parents in her Lamaze class were young married couples. As we all sat together and watched the double-feature movie on epidurals and C-sections, it did occur to Suzanne and me that there might be some suspicion that we were an older, vaguely interesting, lesbian couple. Her suggestion that I ditch the pantsuits and wear only skirts, sling-back shoes, and pearl chokers to the classes apparently did little to dissuade anyone. After her son was born and the two joined a playgroup with the other mothers from the Lamaze class, those mothers informed her that they and their husbands had placed bets on whether or not Suzanne and I were a gay couple.

And of course, if you wait to have your children when you're in your late thirties or early forties, by the time they leave for college, you're in your late fifties. The stumbling block is that after all those years of dressing carefully and modestly so that no teenaged sons' sensibilities will be offended, when your children are actually gone and you can wander about your house in your underwear, you'll be too old and you'll scare the horses. (And the neighbors.)

Actually, more mature parents can be a boon to their offspring, primarily because the memory of middle-aged mothers and fathers begins to fade at about the time their children become teenagers.

When offspring stay out past their curfew, their parents may ground them for a week; with any luck at all, these same parents will forget their child's wrongdoing and promised subsequent punishment. The curfew isn't lifted as much as it's lost from memory.

When my friends and I talk about being pregnant, some of them say they don't want to know the sex of their babies before they're born. What do you think?

I think the excuse for not choosing to learn their baby's gender after amniocentesis or a sonogram—"We want to be surprised"—is ludicrous in this age of information. You'll be surprised whenever you learn the sex, whether you're four months' pregnant or giving birth; you'll be gloriously and sufficiently amazed when you actually see your baby.

One grandmother-to-be said to me, "Finding out the sex of their babies before they're born is all about control. That's what these new parents want over their children." It has nothing to do with control. It has to do with knowledge that is available, and why any parents would choose not to avail themselves of it is more than I can comprehend.

Speaking as a mother who knew the sex of one

child and not the other, knowing was far superior to not knowing. When you can picture a baby girl or a baby boy, rather than a baby, the whole pregnancy becomes more immediate and exhila-rating; you feel closer and more attached to your child before he or she is born. And why would you want a bunch of doctors and nurses and X-ray technicians knowing more about your child than you do?

When I go to baby showers, and the mothers have refused to find out the sex of the babies, all the clothes and bibs are white with yellow ducks on them. They seem to be the most gender-neutral animals. Also at these showers, there's a lot of talk about videotaping the birth. What do you think of that?

I think the videotaping idea was conceived by someone who dropped acid in 1968 and is still tripping. In the first place, who in the world would you show the video to? Your daughter, who would probably take a vow of abstinence and head to a nunnery, or your son, who would probably go ei-ther directly to intensive psychotherapy or to the Federal Witness Protection Program, never to be seen again? You've got your baby as well as photo-graphs and videos. Why would you want a re-minder of your episiotomy?

I agree with you on that one. Do you think when I have a baby that I should try to give birth without drugs? That I should try to keep the whole process natural?

When you had four wisdom teeth pulled, you were unconscious during the entire procedure and then took painkillers. Why wouldn't you also take whatever drugs are offered to make childbirth as comfortable as possible? Enduring pain while giving birth does not make you a better mother, and avoiding pain by taking drugs does not mean that you have failed your baby. It means you are doing the wise and sensible thing.

The *natural* part of being a mother that I find most essential is to nurse your baby. We all know the medical and health advantages of breast-feeding, but it is also the one feature (unless you've found a wet nurse who works part-time at Starbucks) that you can provide for your baby that no one else can. And it's much easier, whether it's the middle of the night or you're on a plane or on the play date with an older child, to nurse your baby than to heat bottles of formula. The time spent nursing your babies is something you'll cherish forever.

For some women, however, breast-feeding proves to be a struggle and if this happens to you, just give your baby a bottle and get on with your life. You haven't failed at anything. Most people my age were bottle-fed and survived. Relatively speaking.

I have one last tip. When you're in your ninth month of pregnancy and you're out and about, always carry a bottle of water with you. Then, if *your* water should break and you find yourself at the grocery store, standing in a shallow puddle in the produce aisle as the other customers stare at you, just point to your bottle and say, "Oh, lord, this must be leaking again." And without further embarrassment, you can grab your cell phone and call your obstetrician.

23

children and stepchildren

Where will you even begin with this topic? You have always had so much to say about the way people raise their children.

➤ Be careful with your birth announcements. Pictures of boxing rings with the legend, "The Little Champ weighed in at 7 pounds, 4 ounces," are as off-putting as cards that proclaim "William, Stacey, and young Will welcome, with joy, the birth of Lily." Hah. Young Will welcomes Lily about as much as he would welcome a blister on his thumb. Let the parents do the welcoming. But do not say, "Will and Stacey welcome, with love, Lily." What else would parents be welcoming a new baby with? Your announcements should say, "William and Stacey Tashjian announce the birth of their daughter, Lily Ames, on June 23, 2004." You can also give the weight and the length, although I don't think that's of any great interest to anyone except her pediatrician and her grandmother.

➤ Name your daughter Tiffany only if you promise to call your son Fortunoff.

➤ Lose any name that requires an apostrophe.

➤ Remember that even though you loved your great-grandmother and great uncle and wish to honor their memory by naming your children after them, Gladys and Cadwell are not names that any child in this century is going to embrace with joy. The class bully or the girls in the cool group will be relentless in using them as often as possible. Tell your children loving sweet stories about their relatives and keep their pictures around, but give those children names that they won't have to explain each time they meet someone new.

➤ Avoid last name–first names, such as Taylor or Lansing. These are more suitable when they either belong to the cast of characters on *All My Children* or are actually to be found on your family tree, rather than pulled up from nowhere. Otherwise, they sound a bit grandiose.

➤ When you and your husband do decide on a name for your baby, do not inform anyone (except me, of course) of your choice until the birth. People feel no qualms about being extremely critical when the name is hypothetical, but once your baby is born and named, you will not hear a peep from anyone about your choice. I wanted a daughter named Emma, even though a close friend told me that in Germany everyone's cook is called Emma. Since I neither live in Germany nor have a cook, I still can't figure out why I also don't have an Emma.

➤ Please don't hang a BABY ON BOARD sign in your rear window. Do parents assume that if they don't announce they are traveling with a baby, other drivers will rear-end their car?

➤ Do not place elastic headbands on baby girls; they do not serve their purpose of keeping hair off the face because babies don't have enough hair for this to be a problem. Try a bonnet. That will keep the sun out of your baby's face.

The same goes for those bows on baby girls with no hair. They scare me because I think they might be glued on to their little heads.

➤ Don't dress them like little adults. They're not. Navy blue is fine for young children but lose the little black dresses and T-shirts. Young boys look like out-of-work saxophone players in double-breasted blazers. Keep your sons in single-breasted jackets until they're taller than you.

➤ Please teach them to be polite. If you allow your children to grow up without manners, you do them an injustice by making them less likable and their lives, in turn, more difficult. If they're well mannered, even if they're naughty, noisy, and carving their initials into compact discs, there will always be some parent or other adult who likes them, because they do say, "Oh, Mrs. Jakobson, I'm so sorry that I have destroyed your entire CD collection of the 'History of Motown.' How can I make this up to you besides writing an extremely remorseful but tastefully appropriate letter?"

➢ When you are complimented on your children's looks, personality, or behavior, please, just smile warmly and gratefully and say thank you. Recently, when I have remarked favorably on children to their mothers, I have been astounded when a few of the women reacted by almost crooning, "Yes, isn't she just the most gorgeous thing. And she's so sweet, too," and "You're right, he is the most wonderful child in the world, so intelligent and just look at those eyelashes." The problem is that this answer leaves the payer of the compliment rather breathless and with no response that makes any sense. Save your understandable pleasure in your children for their father.

➢ Encourage sleepovers. These are delightful opportunities for your children to spend uninterrupted time with their friends, but there is a downside that should be considered. Until my children began spending the night and, unfortunately, the following morning, at their friends' houses, they never knew about hot breakfasts. I had told them only about cold cereal and orange juice, but after a few sleepovers, they began to inquire about scrambled eggs and waffles and bacon. This was a blow to a mother who never mentioned toasted English muffins in front of the children. I had to start getting up fifteen minutes earlier.

➤ If you are having a conversation either on the phone or in person and your child asks you a question, please do everyone concerned a favor and tell your children that it is rude to interrupt people unless the house is on fire or they can't stop the bleeding. If you simply turn to your son or daughter midsentence and leave the person with whom you were conversing talking to no one, you are telling your friend that what she has to say is of little importance, and you are sending your child a message that the world revolves around her or him, that he or she has the power in the family. This is not the secret of successful child rearing.

➤ In this same vein, unless it's a special occasion, don't ask your children what they want for dinner. You're the mother, you're in charge, and it's up to you to make the decision and for them to follow. You're running a household, not a restaurant.

➤ When your child comes home from school, complaining about his teacher, just nod sympathetically, but unless it's an egregiously awful situation, don't take it any further. Children aren't going to like all their teachers any more than they're going to like all their college professors or the people they work for. School is life.

➤ If you adopt a baby, give that child a family name. It's a small gesture, but one that might help make her or him feel more connected to the family.

➤ Do not do your children's homework for them. You can help them with research, teach them how to look subjects up in books and on the Internet, and listen to their ideas, but they are the students, they are the ones being taught and tested and challenged. If they're having a problem, speak to their teachers and let the teachers deal with any issues. You're not helping them learn by reading their books and highlighting the important paragraphs. They have to read everything themselves and learn to separate the significant from the trivial. This is how they learn. Or not. My son once wrote at the end of an English composition, *"My mother assisted me in proof read."*

What about kids who call all adults, and even their relatives, by their first names?

Perhaps the glut of stepparents these days, all of whom seem to be called by their first names, has blurred the line that has historically kept children from addressing adults by their first names, but grown-ups should be called "Mr." or "Mrs." or "Ms." Children must learn that everyone isn't equal, which is why we have titles.

And adult relatives should be addressed by their proper titles. Many contemporary parents seem to feel that Aunt and Uncle and Grandma and Grandpa are outdated designations that are simply too formal, stodgy, and old-fashioned for their children to use; instead, adults in the family are called by their first names. Please make sure that your children don't do this. Don't forfeit a cozy connection for them at a time when families are smaller, fractured by divorce and geographical distance, when parents sometimes must create a family for their children with friends rather than relatives. Using "aunt" and "uncle" is the best way to do this. And, really, who would want to live in a world without Auntie Mame, Auntie Em, or Uncle Remus?

This laxness in using proper titles has the potential to become the nominal equivalent of dress-down Fridays. If Aunt and Uncle are cast aside as if they were Friday's ties and jackets, Grandma and Grandpa are undoubtedly not far behind. What's next on the endangered label list? Mommy and Daddy?

I think that in the same way that some parents feel that traditional schools stifle creativity, they're also convinced that traditional family labels act as an emotional restraint, that children's affections for people are hindered by formality. That is so wrong-headed. Security liberates children.

But make sure that your children don't call their grandparents by their first names. Grandma and Grandpa do provide a special bond, which everyone deserves. Of course, families have different names for these family members. A college friend of mine was known to all as "Dirty," because of the state of his room, his clothes, and his language. His granddaughter calls him "Granddirty." Another middle-aged hippie friend is called "Granola" by her grandchildren. It doesn't matter what they're called but it should be a special grandparent name.

Familial titles can also help to define the relationships in stepfamilies. When you bring a child from a first marriage into a second, and that child can call his stepfather's brother "Uncle Doug," then the child really does become a part of the family.

But what should my future children call my really close friends? Mr. and Mrs. sound so formal.

They can be called Aunt Samantha and Uncle Frank. Your children should understand that grown-ups are not their peers and deserve something more than Samantha and Frank.

Who is easier to raise, a son or a daughter?

I think daughters are easier on their fathers and sons are less work for their mothers. You were a perfect angel until you turned on me at the age of twelve and spent the next ten years informing me that I had lipstick on every one of my teeth. Not to put too fine a point on adolescent behavior, but when I am dressed to go out in the evening, your brother has never looked at me with disbelieving eyes and said, "You're actually going out of the house in that dorky dress?"

Another difference between sons and daughters is when your teenaged son invites friends to spend the night, by the next morning, there will be boys sleeping on couches and in sleeping bags all over the house. Teenaged girls will stack up, seven of them sleeping together in a small room, telling secrets about the seven other girls who didn't make the cut, rather than separate for a night.

Sons don't slam doors. I have seen the floors outside of teenaged girl's rooms. There are often small chips of paint lying about that are the result of a flounce and a bang. After the girls move out of the house, their parents have the halls replastered and repainted.

I asked a friend, who is the head of student relations at a European Study Abroad college program, what she thought were the differences between the boys and the girls. She informed me that for the twenty years that she's held her position, nothing has really changed. The boys can misbehave and get into trouble and be tossed out of the program, but they never moan and whine. The girls, however, have come to her for years with the same complaint: "I have cramps and I hate my roommate."

Girls tell you everything, more than you ever wanted to know, whereas boys tell you nothing. It is entirely possible that your brother has a wife and children, all living down in the storage bin in the basement, but he hasn't felt it necessary to inform me. It's not that boys don't talk, but rather that they don't tell you anything you'd really enjoy hearing about, unless it has been your fondest wish to discuss the Marshall Plan, the Truman Doctrine, and the Soviet SA-11 Gadfly single-arm missile launcher with your son before he goes to sleep. The most personal question one boy ever asked his mother was, "Do you have any stationery that's not mammogrammed?"

In contrast, with a daughter you're always up-to-date on which friend has had her tongue pierced, which teacher is pregnant, and whose mother is getting a divorce because she's having an affair with the football coach. A son only tells you who won the football game. This is not why one has children.

Your son, as well as your daughter, should be able to change a bed, plan, shop for and cook a simple dinner, sew on a button, and iron a shirt and a pair of pants. Don't send either of them into the world without these household skills. If your daughter can't perform these basic tasks, she may have to marry a rich man whom she may not love just so she can afford a cook and laundress, and your son may have to live with or marry someone he or, more important, *you* don't care much about, simply because he's unable to manage his laundry.

During an argument with your teenager, remember that if you lose your temper, your child has won.

Don't give any family jewelry to your daughter-in-law. If she and your son divorce, she'll take

Aunt Mimi's pearl drop earrings with her and give them to her third husband's daughter by his second wife. Buy your son's wife her own earrings.

No matter what the sex of your child is, there are no guarantees in life. One mother I knew had a five-year-old son to whom she devoted long hours reading and discussing the solar system, state capitals, and American presidents. She prided herself on the solid background she was providing for her child until one afternoon when she heard her son's uncle ask, "So what do you want to do when you grow up?"

Her son answered, "I want to eat in the living room."

If my children become homesick at camp, what should I do? I know what you did with me, but I don't know if I'll have the strength.

When your son or daughter goes off to summer camp, is miserable—madly calling you at every possible moment—and desperate to come home, don't allow them to do it. It will simply serve to reinforce the idea that they can't hack it, they cannot stay at camp with the other children, and they feel defeated.

When you went to camp for the first time, you called me at least twice a day in tears, begging me to let you come home, regularly informing me that your appendix was bursting and that you were certain to be in the hospital before the day's end. In desperation, I called the camp director and told him of my plight. He informed me that the minute you hung up the phone after talking with me, you were happy, of very good cheer, and playing with your friends. He said, "If you refuse to take her collect calls, and tell her that she can call you only twice a week, it will be better for everyone. Knowing that she can't call you every day will free her from thinking and worrying about it. And it will be easier on you." When you called that afternoon, I informed you that under the new regime, I would take your calls only twice a week. You didn't seem too upset, probably because you didn't believe me.

The next day the phone rang and the following exchange took place:

Operator: I have a collect call for anyone from Caitlin. Will you accept the charges?

Me: I will accept her call on Wednesday and Sunday. Not until then.

Caitlin: (Wailing) Mommy, please, oh please, talk to me.

Me: No.

Operator: You won't take this call?

Me: No.

Caitlin: Oh, Mommy, I love you so much and I think my appendix is going to burst and I'll have to have an operation. Oh, Mommy, I love you and I miss you and I'm so sad. Please talk to me. I don't want to be in the hospital all by myself. I'm only eleven years old.

Operator: Are you telling me you won't take this call from your poor little girl who is crying and belongs in the hospital?

Me: Yes.

Caitlin: Mommmmyyyyy!

Operator: I don't believe this.

After hanging up the phone, I took to my bed, and lay there crying, awaiting my summons from Children's Protective Services, because I was sure the operator had turned me in. But a custody battle with government agents never materialized; I stood firm and you survived.

The following summer, when you returned to the same camp, you didn't phone me for such a long time that I had to call the camp and make certain that you hadn't stopped off at some nearby hospital to have your appendix removed.

I once heard a guy say that if his parents had allowed him to leave camp when he was homesick, he would never have had the strength to get through his fraternity hazing.

Well, that's heartening.

Is there any one principle that you would like me to take away from all this?

Yes. My advice is to never ignore an opportunity to teach your child a lesson. When your brother was ten years old he posed the following question: "Mommy, if Mussolini were going to die unless someone gave him a kidney and I had the only ones in the world that were compatible, would you let him have one of mine?"

I gave him a reassuring hug and said, "Not if you keep your room nice and neat."

Some of my friends won't leave their children overnight, ever. Not even with babysitters. They say their own parents went out all the time when they were young and they don't want to do the same with their kids. Are they doing the right thing?

The essence of raising children is to do what is right for them, not to react instinctively against what you think your own parents did or didn't do with you. I have a friend who would never leave her two children overnight with either a grandparent or a babysitter because she felt that her own mother left her too often, and she didn't want her children to feel abandoned as she had. That is a case of not thinking clearly. What if you've never left your child and you suddenly break your leg and are hospitalized? If you had left your child in the past, the knowledge that parents do go away and do return would be reassuring. If that same child has to deal with being without her mother, as well as knowing her mother has to undergo surgery, everything is made more complicated.

Raising a child should be a pleasure. It is not as tricky as some of your generation would have one believe. Use your common sense. Of course you and your husband can take trips without your children. They'll cry and carry on when you walk out the door and they'll weep when you call them, but they will survive. As long as you're leaving them with babysitters whom you know and trust and whom they like, or with grandparents or other family members, why wouldn't you take trips? It's important to spend time alone with your husband, because when your children go off to college, it's just the two of you again. As a couple, you should have as much fun and as interesting a life after your children leave your house as you had before they were born.

Your life changes when you have children. And for the better. But it doesn't stop.

stepchildren

Even though she's still pretty young, one of my friends is dating a guy who has two young children from a previous marriage. What is the best way to cope with this situation? I'm asking you because you've had a stepmother and you've been a stepmother. And you'll tell me anyway, so I might as well ask.

The guiding principle in this situation is never to say a disparaging word to the children about their mother. Whine and gripe to *your* friends. That's what friends are for.

If your husband is having problems with his children and discusses these problems with you, just nod sympathetically and listen. Don't add your own criticisms to the mix. It will serve no purpose except to keep him from speaking freely to you about whatever parental dilemmas he's facing. He needs a sounding board, not an echo chamber.

The road to stepmother-hood is often rocky and complicated for everyone involved, including the children. My friend Nell was trying to explain to her six-year-old daughter, Elissa, exactly how she was related to her older half-siblings. "Before I married your daddy and had you," she said, "I was married to another man named Jim, and that's when your sisters, Lucy and Emmy, were born. So Jim is their father."

Elissa seemed lost in thought for a moment and then asked, "Yes, but who is their *mother*?"

Involve your stepchildren in family activities; have fun with them and try to stay as uninvolved as possible in their mother's and father's problems. As long as they have a mother, your role is somewhere between that of a mother's helper and a close family friend or cozy auntie. If you are able to have an amiable relationship with their mother, it will make everyone's lives much more pleasant and satisfying. And it will certainly help move the family birthday parties along.

Be as kind and generous to your stepchildren as you would want *your* children's future stepmother to be to them.

At my engagement party, I recall you gazing around the dining room and announcing, "As I look around and see my three stepchildren and my daughter from my first marriage and then catch sight of my three stepchildren and my son from my second marriage, it occurs to me that I have been married to the fathers of most of the people in this room." If I'd known you were going to say something like that, I'd have given serious consideration to canceling my wedding and eloping.

You mean if I had only spoken sooner, we could have saved the money that we've already spent on this wedding, including a wedding dress that costs more than my parents' first house?

24

and now i'm done

Now that you're heading out on your own, I won't be around to answer all your questions (which is probably why you're leaving), but this book will, I hope, provide you with a basic draft for the new life that you're beginning without me. Knowing the rules will give you the freedom to relax and concentrate on the important issues. Once you've discovered how not to tilt your sofa pillows, you don't have to think about them anymore and you'll be free to read a good thriller, go to a movie, or have microdermabrasion at a spa.

I am aware that we learn more from the bumpy rides than we do from the smooth ones, so during those times that don't play out exactly according to plan, don't lose heart or be discouraged. When a vacation goes horribly wrong and when, after two canceled flights, you finally arrive at your friend's house—where you're to stay for a week— and find the house is unkempt, your hostess is drinking heavily because her boyfriend has ditched her for her sister, and there is nothing in the refrigerator except half a bottle of white wine and some grape jelly, don't think it's all for naught. You'll be hungry but you'll also have a wonderful story to tell for years to come. The only babysitter I remember from my entire childhood was the woman who, after my parents had left for the evening, woke up my younger siblings and me, put us on a bus (the bus driver was her boyfriend), and took us to see a Natalie Wood movie. She got us home and in bed before my mother and father returned; I wouldn't give up the memories of that groggy but thrilling night for anything.

I guess I have to ask this question. Do you have any final advice that you want to give me? Although it's difficult to imagine that you left anything out.

I do have a final piece of advice for you, which I will try to pass on without sounding like the commencement speaker at your college graduation. It is from a psychiatrist I once sat beside on a plane. He said, "When people grow old and look back on their lives, they don't regret what they did, they regret what they didn't do." After that conversation, I realized that for years I had thought that if there was one thing in the world I could choose to do, I would sing. That's when I started up my singing group of five friends who shared my Motown dreams.

And that's when I had to fix dinner because you were rehearsing "Sweet-Talkin' Guy"? Didn't someone suggest that you call your group "The Hot Flashes"?

Oh, she was just jealous. Or younger. We call ourselves "The Glad Girls" and sing at each other's anniversary and birthday parties and once actually had a gig at a charity benefit in a nightclub. Our singing group fills us with sheer bliss and tranquillity. Even though the Ronettes had better hair, the Supremes had better clothes, and the guy who delivers my newspapers has a better voice, we plan to sing into our old age. If I ever come across the doctor I met on the plane, I will tell him that because of his wise words, years from now, I'll probably be begging the other women on my floor at the nursing home to join me in a chorus of "Save the Last Dance for Me." And also, because of him, my regrets are fewer and my life is much more fun.

So, my grown-up girl, marry someone who makes you laugh, vote in every election, and come home often. Even though your old bedroom isn't exactly the same as when you left it—we're converting half of it to a home gym—your old mama is. And she really misses you.

A Mother's Own Advice to Daughters

and one more thing . . .

_____

_____

_____

_____

_____

_____

_____

_____

_____

_____

_____

_____

_____

_____

_____

and one more thing . . .

and one more thing . . .

_____

_____

_____

_____

_____

_____

_____

_____

_____

_____

_____

_____

_____

_____

_____

_____

_____

_____

_____

_____

_____

_____

_____

_____

_____

_____

_____

_____

_____

_____

and one more thing . . .

_____

_____

_____

_____

_____

_____

_____

_____

_____

_____

_____

_____

_____

_____

_____

About the Author

Joan Caraganis Jakobson has written for the *New York Times Magazine*, *Newsweek*, *Town and Country*, *Civilization*, *Cosmopolitan*, *Family Circle*, *Quest*, and an online column for the New York Social Diary. She lives in New York City with her husband and son. Her daughter and son-in-law live eleven blocks away.